How to Become a Real Estate Investor

The Ultimate Beginner's Guide to Real Estate Investing

© Copyright 2019 - All rights reserved.

The content contained within this book may not be reproduced, duplicated or transmitted without direct written permission from the author or the publisher.

Under no circumstances will any blame or legal responsibility be held against the publisher, or author, for any damages, reparation, or monetary loss due to the information contained within this book. Either directly or indirectly.

Legal Notice:

This book is copyright protected. This book is only for personal use. You cannot amend, distribute, sell, use, quote or paraphrase any part, or the content within this book, without the consent of the author or publisher.

Disclaimer Notice:

Please note the information contained within this document is for educational and entertainment purposes only. All effort has been executed to present accurate, up to date, and reliable, complete information. No warranties of any kind are declared or implied. Readers acknowledge that the author is not engaging in the rendering of legal, financial, medical or professional advice. The content within this book has been derived from various sources. Please consult a licensed professional before attempting any techniques outlined in this book.

By reading this document, the reader agrees that under no circumstances is the author responsible for any losses, direct or indirect, which are incurred as a result of the use of information contained within this document, including, but not limited to, — errors, omissions, or inaccuracies.

Table of Contents

Introduction 1

Chapter One: Real Estate 101 3

   The importance of Real Estate Investment Education 4

      Understanding key terms 4

      Adjustable-rate mortgage 5

      Amortization 5

      Appraisal 5

      Assessed value 5

      Buyer's agent 6

      Cash reserves 6

      Closing 6

      Closing costs 6

      Comparative market analysis 7

      Concession 7

      Contingencies 7

      Dual agency 7

      Equity 7

      Escrow 8

      Fixed-rate mortgage 8

      Home warranty 8

      Inspection 8

      Interest 8

      Listing 9

      Listing agent 9

      Offer 9

      Pre-approval letter 9

      Principal 9

      Private mortgage insurance 10

      Real estate agent 10

      Real estate broker 10

- Realtor 10
- Refinancing 10
- Title insurance 11
- Provides access to historical references 11
- Empowers you to see into the future 11
- Helps you make disruptive decisions 12
- Keeps you hungry for more success 13

How to achieve real estate investment education 14
- Books 14
- Mentors 15
- Investment seminars 17
- Newsletters 18
- Webinars 18
- Podcasts 20
- Blogs 21
- Online Courses 22

Chapter Two: Follow Population Trends: Find the Right Area 25
- Look out for areas that are "Down" but with prospects 28
- Seek out cities/places with nearly balanced inflow and outflow 30
- Use the proximity idea as a beginner 32
- Consider your preferred investment area 34
- Think like the tenant/client 37
- Value trumps all! 39

Chapter Three: Investing in the Right Property 43
How to Buy Your First Property 44
- Set your property goals 44
- Find a property 45
- Knowing your ROI 46
- Take a Step 48
- Get an Inspection 49
- Close the Deal 51

Get a Property Management Team... 52
Repeat the Process 54

Before Buying a Property: Note These Signs 55

Exteriors of the property.. 55
The hedges 56
Backyard 56
Outer walls 56
Roof 57
Water Damage 57
Noise Factor.. 59
Ownership History 60
Hidden Areas the Seller Wouldn't Let You See 61
No Permit for Work Done 62
Be Vigilant With Inspection... 63

Chapter Four: Find the Right Real Estate Deal from a Thousand 65

Deals!.. 65

How to Get Real Estate Deals 66

Take a drive around.. 66
So what are you looking for as you drive?....................................... 67
Spread the Word... 68
Use the MLS (Multiple Listing Service) 69
Direct Mail 70
Eviction Courts/Records... 72
Craigslist 73
Online Marketplace 74
Property Management Companies 76
Networking 77

How to know you've Found A Great Deal 79

The area is consistently improving... 79
You found a growing market... 80
The deal meets your long-term investment objectives................... 82

Chapter Five: How to Invest in Real Estate without MONEY! **84**
    OPM (Other people's money) 84
    Joint Venture 86
    Seller/Owner Financing 88
    Lease Option Agreement 90

Chapter Six: The Concept of Sustaining Your Investment Long-Term **96**
    How to Sustain Investments Long-Term 98
        Stay Educated 98
        Diversify your ROI 99
        Be Conscious of Market Trends 101
        Be Resilient 102
        Discover Why You Failed 104
        Experiment with New Markets 105
        Build a Stronger Team 107
        Understand Risks 109
        Utilize the Power of a Network 110
        Be Intentional With Everything 112
        Purchase Facts, Not Emotions 113
        Discover Your Niche 115
        Be an Investor with Integrity 117
        Comprehensive Yearly Plan 118
        Stay Hungry 120

Conclusion **123**

References **126**

Introduction

When you think about investing what comes to mind? Do you imagine long walks on the beach and a family vacation while you earn passive income? Or do you think about the financial freedom you get to enjoy for years to come?

Whatever your thoughts are on investments, one factor reigns supreme; they are the leading most profitable way of building sustainable wealth. There are varying forms of investments, and we will be focusing on a unique platform that has empowered many individuals for years.

Real Estate Investment!

On the surface, it seems like a straightforward concept; a person purchases a house, increases the price, puts it on the market and hopes to make a profit by reselling the property.

But there is so much more to real estate investing beyond buying and selling. When you become a real estate investor, you open yourself up to an exciting investment process with many benefits.

Real estate investing allows you to indulge in your entrepreneurial spirit. You can enjoy tax benefits and build a stable income stream that can be passed from generation to generation.

One of the most striking traits of a great investor is the ability to create a diversified portfolio. With real estate investments, you can build a portfolio that enables you to survive the downside of investing.

One reason to invest in real estate is the appreciation rate that can garner a nice return on investment (ROI). You can flip properties or hold them as rentals. One of the many advantages of real estate investing is that you don't have to live near the properties you own. You can live in the next city, the next state or across country.

Real estate investing has the potential to help the local economy, which in turn can reap some benefits, and it begins with knowing how to stand out in the market. If you seek high-rate returns, you will need to get on board with real estate investing.

The book aims to prepare you with the most effective strategies to launch you into a successful and profitable real estate portfolio. We will explore the most lucrative and safe investments and explore the risks and how to avoid the pitfalls. Read on to begin your journey to success!

Chapter One: Real Estate 101

Knowledge is power and with real estate investing the more knowledge you have, the more successful you can be. You don't need a college education to hold a diverse, performing portfolio; however, knowledge of how the market works and knowing the demographics will help tremendously for making solid investments.

Many interested in the possibility of investing in the real estate market have likely read about Warren Buffet, Tony Robbins and Jason Hartman, all successful real estate gurus. While they each have their own secrets to success, they are cashing in on the most tax-favored asset in the world—income property.

These three real estate gurus, and many more, started at the beginning.

Diving into the market without first learning the how-to's is too big a risk to take, especially if you're investing your retirement fund. You need to be on solid ground and that means knowing everything there is to know about real estate investing.

This book will teach you how to be a savvy real estate investor and build a diverse portfolio without breaking the bank.

The importance of Real Estate Investment Education

Understanding key terms

The first step for new investors is to learn the terminology used in real estate. Adjustable rate mortgage, amortization, appraisal, contingencies, equity, and private mortgage insurance are some of the words frequently used in real estate transactions.

Knowing the jargon is important so when brokering your first deal, everything is understood. Real estate closings can be complicated, with a lot of legal talk and plenty of paperwork to read over and sign. Although most investors have a lawyer to handle closings, you'll still need to sign all the necessary paperwork and understand exactly what you're signing and why.

An example of the importance of understanding the terminology can be found with private mortgage insurance, more commonly known as PMI. This insurance is a monthly premium tacked onto a mortgage to guarantee the loan. PMI insurance is often required when the lender has an average or below average credit score.

If you sign an agreement you don't understand, it can put your investment portfolio in jeopardy, therefore knowing exactly what is said and what is signed is paramount.

The following are words you will frequently hear:

Adjustable-rate mortgage

An adjustable-rate mortgage means the interest rate can change over the course of the loan at five, seven, or ten year intervals.

Amortization

Amortization combines interest and principal into monthly payments, rather than paying off the interest at the start.

Appraisal

An appraiser will determine the value of a home based on a physical inspection of the property. A report is passed on to the lender to ensure the property meets or exceeds the lending price.

Assessed value

The value of a home based on the assessment of the jurisdictional government. The amount of property taxes levied is determined by the assessed value.

Buyer's agent

The person who represents the buyer throughout the transaction.

Cash reserves

These are funds the buyer receives after paying the down payment and closing costs.

Closing

The closing is the last step in a real estate transaction. Final documents are signed, the required payments are made and the keys are transferred to the new owner. This usually takes place in the office of the buyer or seller's agent or attorney. Sometimes closings take place in the office of the county clerk so the deed can be filed at the time of closing.

Closing costs

Closing costs are separate from any required down payment and include title insurance, excise tax and loan processing costs.

Commission

The amount the real estate agent and broker earn from the sale of the property.

Comparative market analysis

The comparative market analysis (CMA) is a report generated on comparable homes in the area to determine a fair market value.

Concession

A concession is a benefit or discount offered by the buyer or seller to help sell a home and close a deal.

Contingencies

This term refers to conditions that have to be met in order for the purchase of property to be finalized.

Dual agency

This is when one agent represents both sides.

Equity

Equity refers to the value of your property that you own. If the property is mortgaged, it's the amount of principal paid. If you have a $100,000 mortgage and paid $20,000 in principal, your equity is $20,000.

Escrow

Escrow is an account that the lender sets up to receive monthly payments from the buyer. Often property taxes are held in escrow.

Fixed-rate mortgage

With a fixed-rate mortgage, the interest rate stays the same throughout the life of the loan.

Home warranty

This warranty protects from future problems such as plumbing and heating, which can be costly to repair.

Inspection

A home inspector will check that the house's plumbing, heating, electrical, foundation, and other features are up to code.

Interest

The cost of borrowing money for a home. Interest is combined with principal to determine monthly mortgage payments. Interest rates fluctuate with the economy.

Listing

A listing is property for sale that's been made public.

Listing agent

The agent represents the seller in the home-buying process.

Offer

This is the initial offer a prospective buyer makes to the seller. The offer may be accepted, rejected, or countered. Another term is purchase offer.

Pre-approval letter

A pre-approval letter that gives an estimate as to how much a bank is willing to lend.

Principal

Principal is the amount of money borrowed to purchase property and does not include the interest.

Private mortgage insurance

As described above, private mortgage insurance (PMI) protects the lender in case of buyer default.

Real estate agent

A real estate agent is a licensed professional who works under a broker.

Real estate broker

A broker is a licensed real estate agent who has met specific criteria to own and operate a real estate business.

Realtor

A Realtor is a real estate agent who is a member of the National Association of Realtors.

Refinancing

To refinance is to re-mortgage property, often to get a lower interest rate or to borrow against the equity.

Title insurance

Title insurance protects the buyer if after the sale it's learned there are liens on the home that the original title search missed.

Provides access to historical references

The best advice you will receive from a successful real estate investor is that historical market statistics are important.

The real estate market trends high and low, and it's also based on demographics. What was a hot investment area ten years ago, might be tapped out. The cost of living also weighs heavily on the market.

It is important to note that you shouldn't solely base any real estate investment on historical data; however, it is relevant for smart investing.

Empowers you to see into the future

There are amazing real estate investor stories that entail an investor making a nice profit from a property that was overlooked by other investors.

A particular area might have been a bad investment opportunity years ago, and is booming today, but now it is much harder to purchase a property at that location. It was those investors who took the risk years ago who will enjoy the benefits.

By learning more about your investments and making moves today, you can get a glimpse into the direction to take for the future.

A regular investor who is not aware of this knowledge and the significance of investment education will make present-hour decisions that are good for today and will likely make him feel good about his decisions. However, such decisions will be irrelevant in the future.

Helps you make disruptive decisions

The ability to make sound investment decisions comes from an upgraded mindset. How else will you know that a particular deal is worth it and another isn't?

When you are always aware of happenings in the market due to your commitment to learning, you will find that you take more calculated risks rather than make impulsive investment decisions.

Disrupting a system means two things:

1. Creating a new pattern of investment that's termed as too "risky" in the market.

2. Modifying an investment system by switching things up with your decisions.

Whichever type of disruption you are willing to take on will be determined by the depth of education you have received. Some investors take the regular real estate investment pathway which entails:

Buying a property—hoping for a good sale—selling it.

If you learn before getting started and continue even after making several investments, you will be known as a disruptive investor.

When you are committed to excellent real estate education, when other investors see a two-year profitability window, you look beyond those two years and seek a ten-year opportunity.

You must get to the level where you strive to be better at investing using new patterns and models instead of what is deemed "acceptable" in the market. Education is the only pathway for disruptive ideas.

Keeps you hungry for more success

An educated mind is an open one, and it is a mind that will not be mediocre because education is empowering.

When investors rush to buy properties in a particular area, you might not be interested because your education has empowered you to know that the profit is not determined by the "rush" but by value.

It is an educated investor who understands the concept of timing with real estate. As you learn, you will become hungry to earn more and achieve more with your investments because you are aware that you can do it.

If you want to remain at the top of your investment game with a hunger for more achievements, you will need to learn more. Learning with this investment platform *never* ends; older investors are still gaining knowledge, so what's your excuse?

Knowing the reason why you should do something keeps you motivated and inspired. Now that you know the "Why," it's time to discover the "How."

How to achieve real estate investment education

Books

You are currently taking the first and most recommended step toward real estate education by reading this book. Books are great for several reasons—they offer you varying insight into what you can expect as an investor in a detailed manner.

More importantly, there are countless books on real estate investment, so when you decide to start reading voraciously, there will always be a book for you.

In this technologically driven age, eBooks are gaining a lot of traction, which means you can read wherever you are and increase your knowledge base with unlimited access to books.

When you finish with this book, you will be hungry for more because the depth of information you get from its pages will help you realize how far you can go by reading more of such content.

Buy books, create a real estate investment library, and if you don't have enough money to buy as many books as you desire, use the library or download a free eBook reader such as the Kindle.

By reading this first chapter, you already have the answers to some questions; the other sections contain profitable ideas you can use as you invest. Imagine all you will achieve as an investor in one year if you can apply all you learn in this book. You will surely experience phenomenal success.

Mentors

In every industry, there are those ahead of you, succeeding and doing well. These are people with experience, and they abound in the real estate investment sector as well.

They could be family members, colleagues, friends, former bosses, former teachers, your neighbor, or someone you met at a party. The goal is to reach out to these people and express to them your desire to learn about investing in real estate.

Let them know how enthusiastic you are to learn and seek their advice on the steps to get started. The suggestions, ideas, or sessions you have with such people will always be priceless because you will be getting experiential and not theoretical knowledge.

Depending on your relationship or rapport with this individual(s), you may be given access to them at any time or have scheduled times to be mentored.

There are numerous reasons why a mentor is an excellent medium for learning, but we can only highlight a few of the ideas here. First, having a mentor enables you to minimize mistakes.

You will be learning from their mistakes, thus avoiding the same kind of problematic situations they experienced (although you will still have your challenges).

Second, a mentor keeps you accountable! The mentor will want to be sure that their time with you is producing the right results. You might have follow-up calls and sessions showing the extent of your progress; this will help you to avoid the pitfalls of mediocrity or giving up easily.

Third, a mentor will grant you access to their educational materials or suggestions that were helpful at the start of their investment journey.

With a mentor, you can ask questions, express your concerns, and be sure of getting answers. You will also get constructive criticism that will reposition you when you are making unimpressive decisions.

When you become prosperous with your investment journey, you will also someday mentor someone else who needs a hand at the start of their investment journey.

Investment seminars

Seminars are a way of getting a face-to-face educational experience if you feel it is what you need. Conferences and workshops are mostly paid events, especially those with reputable experts and investors who are changing the game.

I advise that you attend seminars after getting started with investments for a while because they are a great way to network with other investors and you'll learn plenty of strategic tips that account for market fluctuations.

Although there are some free seminars available, they are mostly organized by real estate experts who want to pitch something to you or sell you on more services.

However, you should invest in seminars conferences and master classes organized by seasoned real estate investors who have been investing for a while with success stories to show for their effort.

If you can afford the cost, seminars can be beneficial to the knowledge you gain and the contacts you make. Many seminars have a nice mix of new and seasoned investors, and you'll certainly meet many interesting people and make new friends.

Newsletters

All you need to receive newsletters is to subscribe with your email address, and you will get relevant information on what's going on in the real estate investment world.

Numerous real estate companies offer newsletters to existing and potential investors that they send out periodically. The best part of receiving newsletters from field experts is that you'll receive the latest most up-to-date market information, and some provide interviews with successful investors.

Before signing up for any newsletter, be sure it's legitimate and from an authority. You don't want your inbox clogged with spam.

Stick to valuable and helpful newsletters that will keep you on your toes as an investor and keep you inspired.

Webinars

Although some webinars are an opportunity for the facilitator to make a sales pitch to you, they can be beneficial, especially at the beginning stages of your investment journey.

If you are a first-time investor, then it isn't advisable to spend a lot of money registering for highly-priced seminars you cannot yet afford, but if webinars can give you the information you seek at this early stage, please utilize it.

Most webinars are free, and they are remote as well, you can take them anywhere you are so long you have access to the platform. Webinars also require minimal time commitment as most of them are between 45-90 minutes.

Webinars focus on a specific topic; you receive insight as to the details of the subject, and it is an effective way to gain mastery over an aspect of real estate faster.

At the end of most webinars, the presenters introduce a Q&A session where you can ask questions, and this is also an avenue to learn from the answers proffered to problems.

Now not all webinars are beneficial, so before you sign up for one carry out a background check on the facilitator. Ask questions about the presenter's qualifications and try to find investors who participated in previous webinars.

If the webinar was highly effective, then go ahead and pay for a more detailed session. Another reason I also advise new investors to use webinars is that it is a platform to get the basic ideas of investing.

Getting ideas from others is one of the reasons why investor education is crucial; if you don't know better, you will use your funds the wrong way. But when you gather bits and pieces of information over a period, you gain knowledge on how to launch into the market successfully.

Podcasts

We live in a fast-paced world. It's sometimes difficult to dedicate yourself to reading the way you would desire. If you can read books, please do, but if you struggle with consistency, please don't give up; you can rely on podcasts.

There is an increase in the demand for podcasts. Lately, it's because people are busy, yet they crave value through the learning process.

You can be carrying out a task while learning how to become a great investor by listening to a podcast. You can tune in while driving in your vehicle and if you miss a part of it, most often you can find archived shows on iTunes or the host's blog or website.

'What's the best part about a podcast? They are free! You will be getting superb content without paying for it, and most podcasts are ad-free as well.

Most real estate experts have podcast channels so you will be gaining access to their wealth of knowledge just by downloading an app or searching iTunes or the Apple shop.

With podcasts, you are exposed to a wide range of perspectives as most podcast hosts interview professional guests. Podcasts are a valuable aspect of the real estate educational process.

Blogs

Whatever you want to learn in life someone has written about it, and it is most likely on a blog.

There are times you will need a long-term course, and then there are times all you need is quick access to information for an immediate situation. Blogs are straightforward, and if you are reading them from a dedicated real estate investment page, you will be getting detailed information.

Blogs are an excellent educational tool because the information will always be there when you need it. So if you read about a particular area on a blog and two weeks later you find that you might have to invest in that area, you can smoothly go back to the blog to retrieve details you will need to make a more informed decision. If you forgot to bookmark the page, you can usually find it in your internet history.

Also, some blog posts are in parts, the topic might be the same, but because it is quite a specific content it's broken down into several posts over several days.

Blogs are also useful because you get to read through comments from other investors, and this is where it gets real. From the comments, you will be able to tell if the ideas shared on the post will be practical.

The comment sections on blog posts will also give different ideas from investors on other aspects of investments and insight on the latest trends.

Online Courses

Online courses are comprehensive and detailed; hence, the reason they are an excellent choice for real estate investment education. There are quite numerous online platforms that offer such courses, and if you want to add more knowledge to what you already know about real estate, you will find them beneficial.

The most powerful feature about online courses is that they help you retain what you learn long-term. Unlike a blog post, you read through once; online courses keep you accountable.

Most courses have a longer duration; they usually cut across several weeks. Most online courses allot you a specific time for completion, and you will be given an assignment or project that is tailored to ensure you fully grasped the lesson.

If you take the assignments seriously, you will internalize the content taught, and it will become real to your experience. Another thing you should note is that online courses can be theoretical and practical at the same time.

Sometimes, you sit back and listen to the facilitator, and there will be sessions when you need to experiment with the theories to test their veracity.

Online courses are like being in class with a teacher; after the duration of the lecture, you will be empowered to use the details you gained to transform your investment experience positively.

So look out for excellent online courses offered by real estate professionals, register for the course, be consistent with the sessions, be active, and get value for your money.

Always seek ways to use what you learn online to your investment processes because that is the only way to utilize the benefits of your education. You can pay for more than one online course at a time as long they are at different times.

Always evaluate your scholarly sources by making certain you are not only getting "predictable" information. Good educational sources will provide recommendations, workable steps, and feedback that will enable you to utilize what you learn.

Real estate education is the building block for success; it will be almost impossible for you to make productive decisions without it. With proper training, you are wiser, and this wisdom causes you to be ahead of others and make good use of your finances for investment purposes.

You have laid a good foundation for your investment experience with education; now is the time to go to the market and take the first step. What does the first step entail? The next chapter has answers, and more!

*Please note that you can also seek additional educational resources from your unique environment if you cannot get access to some of the ideas proffered here. Just don't stop pursuing knowledge.

Chapter Two: Follow Population Trends: Find the Right Area

Real estate education is a consistent process that doesn't end with one seminar. However, learning opens your mind to the exceptional possibilities that lie with your investment decisions.

Here you are, ready to take the first step toward real estate investment. I hope you are excited at the prospect of bringing some of the ideas you discovered in the first chapter to life.

A lot of books and materials often lead investors to get right to the aspect of purchasing a first property. If you did your research on real estate before reading this book, you would probably see "Buy a house" at the top of the list of things you should do first.

However, the truth is that if you make that move without an in-depth understanding of the role played by the area, you will lose out on your investment.

Are you looking for a quick investment get-rich idea? If yes, it will be advisable that you stop reading because you wouldn't find that concept in this book.

What you will find is a step by step approach to investing for beginners that will empower you to build a solid investment foundation. This foundation will become the basis for sustainable wealth creation.

The success of your real estate investment isn't solely determined by the properties you purchase. Take your eyes off houses for a moment and think about the area. It would help if you found a city/street/suburb you like and let that environment be the focus of your investment.

To fully grasp the concept of finding a suitable area, you must embrace the notion of market trends. Markets are always in motion, sometimes they move down, sideways and other times they move up. The concept of market trends is the reason why the stock exchange is always budding with life and activity. Every stockbroker needs to follow the rhythm of the market through its movement (trends).

As a real estate investor you should be proactive about studying the trends in the real estate market to ascertain the best time to make a decision. Great real estate investors do not consider only the trend. You've probably heard the saying, "Location, location, location." A lot of real estate investments are about location.

If you were to do a search of the worst locations for real estate investing, you'd likely return results for the Northeast. With New York and New Jersey being expensive, highly taxed states, they aren't prime locations for a good ROI. Many investors shy away from the Northeast because there's no money to be made.

Weather is another important factor when selecting a location. The Northeast is known for harsh winters. It may be easy to find tenants for rental property, but when it comes time to sell, the cold and snow might keep prospects away.

This is especially so if it's a multi-unit apartment complex. They can be difficult to unload unless they're in an area where there's no harsh weather. They would also need to show a good profit with steady tenancy. Transient tenants place a large expense on the apartment owner as with each exit, the apartment needs to be cleaned, the rugs shampooed, etc. This can add up, especially if you're an absentee landlord paying a property manager.

All these considerations should be explored before signing a purchase offer.

A vital lesson you must consciously uphold as an investor is to think like your prospective clients. Market trends inspire prospective buyers to jump when interest rates are lowest.

With the stock exchange, it is difficult to predict the market trends, but this isn't the case with real estate. The market trends with real estate tend to move at a slower pace, and if you follow it keenly, you will know when it's the best time to invest and what areas hold out the most ROI.

A city that had impressive growth last year will most likely have the same growth manifested this year and a higher growth projection next year. On another hand, an area that didn't do so well in the market last year isn't doing well now and likely won't next year.

By following the trend (and in addition to other factors we will discuss subsequently) as an investor, you can tell which city or area will do better in the future.

You should also know the reason why you are reading all sides of market trends (up, down and sideways) in this chapter. The idea is so we can shatter the popular yet erroneous concept that real estate investors should only invest in areas that are doing better. Which is when the properties are "Up" (we will elaborate on this idea and correct the impression shortly).

Remember, at this point, we are not talking about investing in a *property,* we are focused on an *area* so keep that in mind as you read on.

Look out for areas that are "Down" but with prospects

A popular trend for real estate investors is to seek out areas that people are moving into because it will guarantee high returns. There is nothing wrong with this trend; it streamlines the investor's choice to only the areas with a steady population.

There is an immense possibility for ROI in areas that are down as well. We want you to be a very knowledgeable investor, and we advise that you also consider "down" areas that have prospects for colossal returns.

In addition to your search for areas, clusters of streets, suburbs or anywhere else with increasing population, note the areas that have been down for a few years and suddenly spring up into becoming the first-choice for people.

The real estate trick is to find the area at the bottom and know when it will take off. For such down areas the prices are low, which means you get to buy at a low price and when it gains prominence you rent, lease, or sell at a higher price.

A major mistake most investors make is buying when the area is at the top, which could be very expensive. At those high times, the sellers are taking advantage of the population rush.

Always remember the three trends of all investment markets:

Upward, sideways, and downward.

If you ever buy upward, you will need to sell that way too to get returns. You can also sell sideways (just a little profit) or downward (sell at a loss).

However, if you focus on down areas with potentials, you will only make sales upward after investing. This pattern means that you must be conscious of the areas with regard to their upward and downward trends.

So is an area going upward? Downward? Alternatively, sideways?

When you make investment choices think about these trends and make purchases that will give you high returns long-term. Ignoring the downward trends will deprive you of the opportunity to gain revenue from suitable investments.

Some areas will give you insight into the kind of experience you will have with your investments. As such, you must pay attention to what you are getting from the area.

Make your choices based on the data you get from researching the areas of interest to you. Some other areas may have issues being on the upward level because of a few challenges in the environment.

The problems with such areas could be the roads, street lights, or any other challenge that will affect the quality of the experience for those who buy properties in that area.

For some areas, the government is responsible for the changes, and if you sense that there will be a commitment from the government in the near future, go ahead and invest.

Don't wait until the positive changes occur before buying. If you buy when prices are up, there will be many investors rushing to jump on the investment train, and you would have to buy beyond your investment plan.

Seek out cities/places with nearly balanced inflow and outflow

When considering an area, you will have to do a lot of thinking and data research. A prominent data you must become aware of is the balance between inflow of people into the area and the outflow.

The keyword with this idea is "balance," and you should know that there is never a perfect balance with this idea because people move in and out of an area based on personal decisions.

So what you should look for is the nearest data to balance that shows how often people buy/rent properties in that area and how often they move on as well.

This data is crucial because it will enable you to settle for an area that goes through the predictable real estate up/down trend but still managed to remain relevant through time.

At some point, an area that remains on the upward level may experience a sudden shift with people moving out.

You should also monitor the duration of the tenants' leases or rents in that area as well; this will be the determining factor for inflow/outflow.

People move in and out of an area for various reasons. If you live or invest in a college town, students come and go frequently. However, it's important that you don't discount a college town as an investment opportunity as, depending on the laws of the community, you can rent a house to several students and charge a per student rate that is almost equivalent to renting to one person or one family. For example, if the local government codes allows rental of a four-bedroom house with six occupants, each student can be charged $600 per month, netting you $3600 every month school is in session.

Also remember to check the schools, churches, community centers, places to go, etc. when researching an area.

Use the proximity idea as a beginner

Another step you can take toward finding a functional area is to seek out an investment option you can easily access at any time. Big-time investors may not have to visit every area they consider for investment. Such successful investors have impressive ROI and agents that work with them, bringing investment briefs.

These "Big" investors rely on their experience and the people they work with to make decisions. But as a beginner, you will most likely have to do most of the searching and decision making yourself, which is why you have a detailed manual with this book.

There are a lot of areas you can consider for investment purposes, but try to stick to areas that are within reach for you. At this stage, you don't have the financial capacity to travel from one state to another to review a property.

Traveling for all investment opportunities will cause you to focus on prospects instead of concrete ideas.

Whatever area you settle for that will be your investment choice is undoubtedly within reach from you, try to seek it out. A very successful investor once advised beginners that they should buy their fundamental properties from places they can jog to quickly.

When you have chosen an area (you will learn how to make this choice below), visit the city and ascertain if it is a perfect fit for the idea you have. It has to be a place where you can quickly go to just in case there is an emergency or if you need to fix a problem.

Find an area that is close to your home because, at this stage, you are bound to make mistakes. You would spend even more money trying to fix the errors when the investment property is far from home.

You might ask what if there is an area that has truly great prospects, but it is far from home? What can I do? There are two things you should consider:

1. Being confident that an area will give you high returns isn't enough to take the risks of it being so far away (At this beginner stage). It might look good on paper, but what will you do if you don't get a tenant or buyer?

2. You can go ahead to secure the area and take your first significant investment risk.

So you need to be *certain* before making the decision. Don't go with projections if you are going to stick to a property that is far off. In addition to the predictions, find out if there are ready buyers or tenants within a short timeframe.

You don't want to have a property in an area that is too far off for you to maintain.

Consider your preferred investment area

There are different aspects of real estate investments: retail properties. Commercial, industrial, residential, etc. For you to succeed with this first step, you must know your preferred investment area.

When you know the area you are interested in, you tend to develop a laser focus on deals, news, and trends in that chosen area.

Now you can have more than one area of interest as an investor, but they should all be clearly defined.

There are two kinds of investors, and you will know who has an increasing tendency to succeed at a faster rate.

The first type of investor doesn't have clearly defined interests in areas for investment purposes. They will invest in any market at any time and without prior information on how the market works.

The second investor has an array of interests in multiple areas, but he is *aware* of his choices, which makes it easier for him to become intentional about his investments.

Both investors are dealing with their investments based on the kind of real estate education they have. If you followed the content of the first chapter, then you will know that the second type of investor is the kind you should become.

Why should you be intentional about your investment area of choice?

If you don't have choices, everything will look like an excellent prospect for you. But the problem is that you will be led to make uninformed choices that can lead to significant loss.

You've got to know *what works for you!*

Let's head back to the stock market for some investment lessons, shall we?

A person who is most successful with his/her investment in stocks always knows the kind of shares to buy. Some of these investors will tell you they prefer to purchase the stocks of blue-chip companies (this is an example). So even when they buy one or two stocks from other companies, occasionally their primary focus is on blue-chip companies.

Before such investors settle for blue-chip companies, they have spent time observing the market and the performance of various companies in the stock market.

These investors also realized that blue-chip companies in the stock market are long-lasting organizations that offer profitable returns. So this investor has his eyes set on all kinds of information, news, and every other thing that feeds him details about blue-chip companies.

Meanwhile, the other investor without a clearly defined path or choice of investment area will have to try to listen to *all* real estate investment news.

Your next question is how you are going to know that the area you will focus on is the right one?

As a beginner, you are at an exciting phase of your investment journey—a stage where you get to test the markets to find out what works for you. Don't try to rely on another successful investor's choice. That accomplished investor was once a beginner who took risks trying out areas to invest in, lost money, and learned lessons the hard way before getting a firm grasp on investing.

You can start by observing the fields available to you, studying their history, past performances, market trends, etc. The time you spend studying the areas will help you narrow it down to a few great options you can invest. But it shouldn't stop at observation or research.

Take a step further with all you have learned in this chapter to invest in one of the areas and watch how it turns out. Experience in the market is what teaches you as an investor.

The theoretical aspects that entail learning about markets are meant to show you what it looks like and what "Could" happen.

You only learn what happens when you take calculated risks.

So dedicate time to research on profitable areas, and ask questions about the investment process from those who are currently investing.

Think like the tenant/client

A real estate investor caters to the needs of those who want to own their home to entrepreneurs who need offices, leased buildings, etc. All of these varying property needs revolve around an area, street, city, etc.

If you are going to turn your potential deals into closed deals, you will have to start thinking like your clients. For you to succeed with this step, you must handle the level before this one, which is knowing your choice of investment area.

Think critically about the area to choose if you are still unsure of this concept: it is a vital part of the process when you go to the different areas to check out investment options think about the client—the moment you see the field, think about the person leasing or renting the property.

You are not supposed to know the area as an investor; at this point, view the environment as though you are going to make a personal purchase. What do you think of the street? Is it impressive? If you are going to invest in homes for families, do you think their kids would love the neighborhood?

You need to ask these questions and be truthful with your answers so you can relay the value of the area to potential clients when you get a deal.

Another way you can ensure the best interest of your investment from a client perspective is to research what they want in an environment, city, street, or area.

For real estate investors who invest in highly-priced, luxurious properties, they need to get details beyond the property itself. The wealthy individuals who buy such properties consider the area before the structure.

If you want to become an investor who specializes in properties for ultra-rich individuals, then you must consider the area through their eyes. Such people crave privacy with hidden homes for security purposes.

If you place a property on the market with an easily accessible area, you will not attract the kind of buyers or tenants you want. Even if you have an agent later who helps with meeting clients, you must make it your duty to know everything about your investment. Knowing everything enables you to hit your targets and get your returns.

If you are going to lease a property to a manufacturing company, for example, you need to consider the area and how it favors the production process of the company.

Can they get their raw materials quickly? Are the roads properly interconnected to aid deliveries?

If a particular area isn't good enough for the real estate sector you are focused on, then don't invest. Do not assume that someone will ignore the glaring disparity between the area and the property.

Your choice to ignore the needs of your tenant or buyer and make an investment even when it doesn't seem right will affect your returns long-term.

Value trumps all!

As an investor who seeks to maintain relevance in the real estate sector, one word must be everything to you, value! Of course, you are going through the process of learning and investing to generate profit, but then the cost is a magnet for increased revenue.

When searching for the perfect area, be motivated by the desire to only settle for an area that is of value, not just to you but to the people who will buy, rent or lease the property.

One of the common mistakes beginners make is to seek out areas that are valuable to them. So they go all out, checking out places that suits their idea of an appropriate environment.

The problem with this idea is that what you consider valuable may not have the same interpretation for your tenants or buyers.

This disparity means that the concept of value to a real estate investor has a dual function.

Settle for areas that hold such a valuable appeal to potential clients that they are willing to adjust their budget for your property.

When considering the value proposition, stick to finding areas to invest in that will boost returns on your investment. What are you seeking? Seek out a more significant percentage of your investment that the target group will love.

Seek out areas that give companies visibility if your choice of real estate investment is in office spaces, office lease/rentals.

The area has to be well laid out for "offices" to thrive and not for residential homes. When you visit a city with what you are looking for in mind, try to find the value even before you find a property.

Some real estate investors flip the process by first finding the property. The problem with this choice is that even if the property fits the description of what you seek if the area is not valuable, you will have a hard time selling it to anyone.

Using our example with company offices, when you find a property with well-structured offices and everything else, you take the next step forward to invest, right?

But if the area is too difficult to access using any means of transportation, you would have a failed investment in your hands. Two things will happen: first, you will either undersell, lease, or rent the property (because it has no value to the client). Second, you will leave the property while hoping that someday the accessibility challenge is fixed.

Regardless of your choice between both options, you will lose!

To avoid losing out, you must be keen on value. Investors who are poised to invest in valuable areas tend to be selective when certain offers are made to them because they understand the arithmetic of investment.

It isn't about making ten deals in a year that require you to slash your price list and having little or no ROI. Successful investing is about the three deals you executed flawlessly with an increased ROI and a powerful reputation in the industry.

Value is crucial. Valuable areas don't sell faster, yet they secure more funds for the investor. As a beginner, I can understand the urgency you feel to start earning from your investment. But if you only want to make money, then settling for any area is excellent.

However, if you are inspired to create a real estate investment solution that adds value to your experience, then do this: seek out areas that are beyond regular/ordinary.

When you are building a sustainable venture, you don't rush off to get things done; you take your time to watch things unfold. The difference between an average real estate investor and a successful one is that the latter isn't in a hurry to invest while the former wants to put money out there as quickly as possible.

You are not going to be an average investor, so you are built up to see beyond the "Hottest selling properties" of the moment. Instead, you should make decisions backed by the reality of market trends.

Now you have the perfect area, you have made significant progress and ready for the next step, locating and investing in the right property!

Chapter Three: Investing in the Right Property

After getting a suitable area, the next step you should take is to locate your property of choice. We are midway into this journey, and we should handle this part of your investment *now* because you have the right set of information to locate the property.

Buying a property is a process in itself because there are some critical aspects you will have to consider before releasing funds; you have to know what you are doing.

Due to a lack of information on how to properly invest in a property, some investors give up quickly, and it shouldn't be the case with you. If you know what to do, even when you make mistakes, you will find ways to make the investment process run smoothly.

This chapter is an efficient section as were the previous chapters. You've got to take action and implement what you discover so you can gain increased experience as a real estate investor.

Now, this chapter will provide insight into two significant parts of investing in properties.

The first part will take you through the process of BUYING, what you should do when you are ready to invest.

The second part will be about the WARNING SIGNS or things you should look out for before buying a property.

So are you ready to get started? Everything you've learned builds up to this point: buying your first property!

How to Buy Your First Property

Set your property goals

The first step to take to buy a property is to define your goals. The mistake some investors make is to go into the market without set goals, so they tend to make mistakes because they don't even know what they want.

In curating your goals, you will need to ask a lot of questions:

- Do I want to invest across state lines?
- What kind of property do I want?
- How many properties can I acquire within the next six months?
- Why am I investing? (Crucial question)
- What is my target ROI?
- Do I want to have tenants or sell off immediately?

Make sure you write down the answers to these questions. You can add more considerations that give an insight into what you seek on this real estate investment pathway.

You will also observe that as time goes on, your goals get modified to suit the reality of the market. If for example, you wanted to invest in a particular area but after researching you find that the area doesn't have as much potential as you thought, you can make a switch to another city, street, district or state.

But you need to set goals to know all of the changes that take place within an area. If you get it right with this first step, you will surely get every other aspect right because the entire search for a property is for it to be in line with your goals.

If you don't set goals, you will wander into the market and feel lost; you will settle for any property that "seems" like a good deal and lose money in the process.

Find a property

Your goals are out; next is to find a property that matches the description of your goals. You have a specific market in mind so you can contact a real estate agent in that market that can get you the exact property you seek.

Let the Realtor know your investment intentions, how much you want to spend, and the number of properties you wish to acquire in a single or multiple transaction style.

You might have to go through a few Realtors before finding the one that suits your investment goal and is committed to making it happen. You don't need a Realtor who is only concerned about the money (realtor commissions); you need someone who understands the importance of your goals.

You can bypass Realtors by searching for properties on your own that match your goals and your ROI expectations. The truth is that you will get a high return on investment when you are creative with your property approach.

Chapter four of this book will give you a list of plausible ways to find properties on your own. You don't have to rely on a Realtor if you don't want to deal with one.

Knowing your ROI

Why are you becoming a real estate investor? It is because of returns on investment, which is why you must know how the profits are going to turn in while keeping a keen eye on your numbers.

The buying process is not about how cute the property is or the beautiful grass out front; it is all about breaking even and getting a high return for your investment.

You've got to know the numbers you seek first, so sitting down with a real estate agent is crucial. Make your goals very clear by stating what you expect as returns.

For example, you can categorically state that you wouldn't consider a property that doesn't give you a 15 percent ROI. So when the real estate agent sends you property briefs or when you find properties on your own, you will only focus on the ones that have the potential of giving you nothing less than the 15 percent ROI you seek.

You've got to know the amount of money you will be letting go and the added amount.

Here's an illustration on how you can calculate ROI on cash to a cash transaction, the figures below are all examples to buttress the point.

How to calculate ROI on cash investment transactions

If you've got $50,000 in your bank account and you want to use it to pay upfront for a property you need to ask the profit margin on that $50,000.

For you to calculate your ROI, you've got to know how much you will be charging the tenant for monthly rent. So assuming your place rents at $800 per month, that will be $800 X 12 months of the year = $9,600.

The $9,600 is the gross rent for the year. It doesn't stop here; you have to divide the total with the cost of the house ($50,000) and get a percentage of your ROI.

Now the illustration above is not peculiar to all real estate calculations for ROI; it is a way of showing you how to calculate and also express the importance of being aware of your ROI at all times.

Remember that you will need to factor such things as property repairs, maintenance, and taxes. In the end, you should still be able to get a substantial income from your investment that will motivate you to go for more.

Take a Step

When you've figured out the numbers and your ROI on the property, you need to take action. The actionable step you take speaks of your commitment to the property. As a first-time investor, when it is time to release funds, you will surely have cold feet because, despite your checks, you want to make sure that you are making the right decision.

But you've got to know that you will never be 100 percent certain; this is one of the earliest lessons you will have as you continue to invest. You will never have that certainty.

If you want to wait to be 100 percent sure, you will never take action and excellent properties will slide past you. So 80 percent assurance is good enough. When you are 80 percent sure of the deal, go ahead and take the plunge.

What matters at this point are your numbers; if they are in synch and you've got your projections about the property right then you need to take a step.

Another consideration you need to take action is the property goals you set with the first step. If the property and the entire investment process aligns with your goals, then you should invest.

As a beginner, you should know that your knowledge of the market at this point is theoretical, which encompasses what you've studied in this book and other forms of real estate education.

The real action takes place when you start investing, and that is where EXPERIENTIAL KNOWLEDGE comes into play. The steps you make now will be the experience you bank on when you have several other deals later.

Get an Inspection

When you make an offer that interests the seller, you will have to conduct a thorough inspection of the property. Ask questions and don't be shy about pointing out any flaws you see. You're making the investment and you want to be certain it's a sound one.

It would behoove you to hire a property inspector to at this juncture to ensure there are no major repairs needed. As previously noted, the inspector will check the plumbing, heating, electrical, roof, staircases, chimney and any other structural issues. Be sure to use a licensed inspector. If your real estate agent can't recommend one, often the local fire department will have a list of reputable inspectors.

Any problems found by the inspector will need to be repaired by the seller, especially if mandated by the lender. The inspection protects both you and the bank. A typical inspection will cost approximately $300 on up, depending on the size of the dwelling. The cost has to be paid upfront (it can't be rolled into the mortgage), but it is well worth the cost.

You should know that regardless of your prior decision about investing in the property, during the inspection, you might have a change of mind. Be as objective as possible by avoiding an emotional attachment to the property. Should the seller refuse to make repairs or alterations, you can withdraw your purchase offer.

If your lender is giving you an FHA or other government loan, some repairs must be made by the seller. An example of this would be a stairway with no railing. The lender will require the seller to add a railing at no cost to the buyer or the bank. A re-inspection will be necessary to ensure the work was done to satisfaction.

The inspector will provide you with a report that details the condition of each structure and utility that was inspected.

When you weigh everything as well as the value the property

brings, and it meets to your satisfaction, then you are ready to take the next step. Closing the deal!

Close the Deal

After the inspection and your reviews, your decision will be obvious: to buy or not to buy. If you go with the former, then you will have to close the deal, and that is how you buy your first property.

Congratulations!

When you submit a purchase offer, it will have an approximate closing date and a date by which the closing must take place.

As the closing process begins, there will be many people involved and it can become frustrating. But hang in there because in the end, the closing will go smoothly.

Your real estate agent and lender will keep you apprised every step of the way. You might go a week or two without hearing anything, but don't worry. No news is good news.

The last and most important step falls with the underwriter. This is the person who underwrites the loan to ensure everything is good and that nothing's changed in the 5-8 weeks it takes to close.

A final credit check will be run, and any changes to the negative could impact your interest rate. It's best to refrain from utilizing any credit until you've closed.

On the day of the closing, you'll need to have a bank cashier's check for your down payment. Personal checks aren't acceptable.

There will be a lot of documents to sign so be prepared for that. A closing can take up to two hours. If you don't attend the closing, your lawyer will and you'll have to make sure you're available by phone should any questions arise.

You will have access to the property when the seller receives all fees. Unless special arrangements were made, you will take possession at the closing. You should receive the keys and any other necessities such as a garage door opener, security system passcode, and utility building keys.

Get a Property Management Team

It is pertinent to note that the path of a real estate investor is about positive and negative moments. The negative moments are due to mistakes. However, we must look at minimizing such errors by taking the right steps even as beginners.

So this means that you will need help!

Finding an excellent property management team is crucial. The team will handle the responsibility of carrying out tasks that will guarantee the integrity of the investment process and the state of the property.

Property management teams will run background and credit checks on your prospective tenants. They will check for eviction notices, relationships with previous landlords, payment history, etc.

The property management team will also collect the rent checks on your behalf and take care of your property. If you are living in a different state from your investment, then you will need a team such as this to keep tabs on the house with consistent maintenance.

A good management team will also ensure that the property is rented, especially at the initial stages of your purchase. You won't have to go looking for tenants or wondering if you have the right tenants.

Find a good team. You must find one you can work with and an organization that focuses on your long-term interests. More importantly, be mindful with regards to paying the team.

Don't use teams that drain you financially. Before partnering with them, make sure you understand their charges. For example, if a property management team charges $50 to check if there are leaves on the lawn after a massive windstorm, they are not the right match for you.

Before signing any contracts, be sure you check the reputation of the property management team and know the terms. Ask how they will submit invoices for work performed. You want to be sure you'll receive itemized invoices and that any work done inside a tenant's premises will be signed by the tenant to ensure the work was actually done.

A management company will do such tasks as mowing lawns, trimming hedges and exterior painting. Make sure the work is actually being done by requesting pictures. Don't be afraid to ask. Remember, they work for you!

Repeat the Process

Have you ever heard the statement "Rinse and Repeat?" That statement refers to the art of doing something that is proven to work when repeated.

The above steps are a guide for your first investment process. At the end of the process, which signals the concluding part of the deal, you will want to invest again.

Investors love the thrill of being in the market. The fun doesn't stop even when some lose money with unpredictable transactions. They know that the only way to get better at it is to be consistent.

So repeat the entire process when you are ready for the next investment cycle. Start from the beginning until the last part. A significant thing that will feature prominently is the fact that you will begin to make improvements with the process.

Don't sit on the laurels of your first successful transaction; go for the second, third, and fourth. Take on the entire process again as if you are doing it for the first time. Start renovating your next property and remain active as an investor in the market.

The more you repeat the steps here, the higher your chances of getting better. However, you should know that not all transactions are the same. You will start to notice the differences in the market after your first investment.

The observable differences mean that for some transactions, you may not have a book to guide you through the process. But what you will have is your intuition. As you read, your mind is being sharpened to become increasingly conscious of how to make good deals.

When faced with a tough investment choice after your first successful investment, in addition to all you've learned, listen to your self-developed real estate instinct. Try to discern when something is off about a deal even when it looks good on paper.

Before Buying a Property: Note These Signs

Exteriors of the property

The surfaces of a property are the first parts of the building you see, and if you are not vigilant enough, a lot can miss your eye. So we will break down the parts you should be intentional about checking:

The hedges

Look out for fake hedges! Some sellers spray their fences, get artificial grass for the unkempt lawn, and do other things to boost curb appeal. If a seller is doing all of these to impress you, then it means that there are other hidden things as well.

The goal for an inspection is not to see a perfect house but to see a real one. The seller has to be truthful about every aspect of the house, so you know what you are buying before committing to the transaction.

Backyard

The backyard is part of the exterior you need to inspect. A poorly kept garden sends a clear message on a lack of maintenance on the part of the owner.

Even if the seller cleaned up the backyard nicely before you showed up, if you are observant, you will know if something is amiss.

Outer walls

Without stepping a foot into the main house, the exterior walls can give you all the information you seek. Are there cracks?

Mold? Signs of leaks? Does the building generally look too old? Does it seem like there was an effort to maintain the walls?

Vigilance is essential because when you need to get your ROI, it will be a factor.

Roof

Don't overlook the ceiling; it is also an essential part of the property. You don't want to buy a property with a leaking roof. Ask the seller about the state of the roof. Does it leak when it rains? Are their ceiling stains to indicate there had been a leak? If so, was the roof repaired? Most importantly, ask how old the roof is and if there's a transferable warranty on it.

Water Damage

Nothing spoils a building more than water, and it can affect the foundation of the building. A significant sign to look out for before buying a property is water damage.

Unlike some other forms of damage easily concealed, the damage caused by water is glaring, but you have to look for it. Some sellers may try to hide water damage with paint.

So, when you study the property look at and touch the walls. Even if you repaint the property after buying it, you will spend more money to fix the damage caused by water.

The moisture trapped in the walls will lead to mold on the walls, which can cause allergies. There are two types of mold to watch for. Black mold, which is difficult to remove and often returns if it's not professionally removed and green mold, which is a sign that there had been a recent water seepage or too much humidity inside. Both should be warning signs that the property might have some major expenses down the road.

In addition to the walls, check the base of the bathtub and the toilets. A significant area that shows you water leaks and damages in the property is under the windowsills. If you spot warped sheetrock by the windowsills, it means there is a water leak somewhere. Be sure to check for rust around drains as well.

If you notice these issues with the property and you still want to buy it, ensure that the seller fixes the problems. Also, make sure the changes are done right before you buy so you aren't bearing the cost later. Also, be sure to get it in writing if the seller agrees to the repairs.

It's important to note that no matter how much you love a place, and no matter how excited you are to own it, don't show it in the presence of the seller. If you appear overly eager, the seller might try negotiating the cost of repairs with you. The seller should be made to feel if they don't make the repairs, you'll walk away.

Keep in mind, most sellers are willing to invest in repairs to make the sale. The longer real estate has been on the market, the less chance it will sell.

Noise Factor

When you visit a property, you may not get all the details you seek in one day. Your inability to fully grasp every aspect is the reason investors are advised to visit the property more than once at varying times.

Noise is one of the least concerns of investors, but it is a big deal. Some sellers may not be open about the effects of noise on the property because they want to sell hastily.

Drive down the street at night to determine if it's a quiet neighborhood. Check out the nearby buildings. Are there taverns in the neighborhood? Concert grounds? Fast food joints or restaurants? Make a mental note of everything you observe that could impact the noise level. Remember, most municipalities have noise ordinances so be sure to check the times for loud noise. Many municipalities have the information on their websites and if not, a quick phone call will garner the answer.

Noise level is essential because when you want to resell this property, the buyers might be concerned about this factor. If you take on a property located in a noisy place, you might end up having to sell at a reduced price.

The property's proximity to the airport might be valuable to tenants who love to travel but often is a problem for those who want a peaceful area. Trains and bus stops can also be a hindrance as can a busy street that allows tractor trailers to travel on them. Conversely, you might find tenants who don't own vehicles and want to live on a bus line or other mass means of mass transportation.

Ownership History

When you buy a property, there is no going back! You take full responsibility, which means that if the previous owners had issues with the house without informing you, it all becomes your challenge.

No property is perfect. We are only advocating for fewer problems within the first few years of purchase, which is why you need to check ownership history before buying.

If the same property is listed over and over, it usually means that the previous owners are running away from something.

Of course, no one expects a person to own a home for a protracted period. But if you loved your home, you wouldn't be running off to sell it after a few years, right?

More importantly, if the person who buys it from you does the same, it will continue with every buyer. Soon enough (if you buy the property) you will realize that there is a problem with the street or the house itself.

If you buy that property, you will also have difficulty selling it because it has a questionable ownership history already.

Hidden Areas the Seller Wouldn't Let You See

When considering a property, be mindful of the seller's ease of access. Some sellers have nothing to hide, so they will willingly let you in and give you the liberty to look through at will.

But for sellers who have not been honest with you from the start about the actual state of the property, they will be evasive with your questions. They might prevent you from entering individual rooms.

As an investor; you also need to become sensitive to how people act. Evasiveness from sellers is one of the reasons why some investors send agents or professional house inspectors to check out properties. Realtors and inspectors can most often tell when a seller isn't genuine from the first interaction.

But if you don't have access to such persons or cannot pay for them, you should be very observant. Insist on viewing every aspect of the house, and if the seller shows even the slightest hesitation, then it means something isn't right.

One of the significant areas often overlooked by investors is the basement. So an inauthentic seller can have a messy basement and sell the property without the buyer knowing anything.

The attic is also another place you shouldn't ignore. Make sure you go through the entire property without assuming that because it all looks good on the outside, then it is right on the inside.

The seller shouldn't prevent you from looking in the backyard or even checking the roof. You must be clear from the beginning: complete access or no deal!

No Permit for Work Done

For you to be a thorough investor, there are some documents you must request from the seller, and one is a permit for work done on the property.

You should ask for these permits so you can ascertain if the work measures up to the standard code with building rules in that state.

You will surely get a definite default answer from some sellers when you ask about the changes done to some parts of the house. But if the seller is not truthful, you wouldn't know hence the reason for proof of work (permit).

Such permits are the 3R report, which is the Report of Residential Building Record. The document is akin to a report card for a property. Every change/additions done on the property is on the report card.

If the seller speaks of an extended balcony, then it should reflect on the report. If there is no mention of an extended gallery, then there is a higher chance that the balcony (if done at all) wasn't up to standard.

Now you wouldn't need a permit for every single change done to the property. For example, you wouldn't need the documents for changes in the bathroom or a change of blinds at the window.

You only need permits for significant work that cut across electrical and structural alterations that will affect the house long-term if not done the proper way. If the building was rewired a few weeks before the inspection, you need to get all the details. If you don't ask for the permit and there is an electrical fault that leads to a fire accident after buying the property, it will be on you!

Be Vigilant With Inspection

It can't be stressed enough how important it is to be vigilant with the inspection. It's critical that you look beyond the obvious and even what the building inspector noted. Now it's time to put your eyes to work.

What do you see? When you look in the bathroom, do you see mildew? Do you see cracked caulking?

If there's a fireplace, does it look well-maintained? Does it look clean? Ask the owner when it was last swept.

Don't forget to check all stairways. Squeaking stairs could mean there's some structural damage.

Open cupboard doors and drawers. Do they open and close

effortlessly? Are there any signs of mouse or bat droppings?

While on the subject of rodents, look for signs of them in every room. You don't want to purchase a dwelling that has an infestation of bats. They can be awfully hard to remove.

If you are not willing to spend a lot of money on renovations, then you must take inspections seriously.

Well, there you have it! A complete guide for purchasing your first property. You have shown impressive resilience thus far, and if you express the same dedication to your investments, you will surely succeed.

Chapter Four: Find the Right Real Estate Deal from a Thousand

After reading through chapter three, you will probably feel like you have a good handle on real estate investing.

While it's great that you can get real estate education and know how to get the right area and properties, you should also discover how to secure what makes all of these ideas possible for you.

Deals!

Every market presents opportunities for its participants, but the possibilities are not kept somewhere for the investors to take when they need it. Investors need to actively search for these opportunities, which are deals, and then use them to boost their investment experience.

We will achieve two objectives with this chapter:

The first aim is to introduce you to a myriad of ways you can get real estate deals.

The second objective is to teach you tips on how you can identify a good deal.

As a beginner, it is quite understandable that you want to get as many deals as possible because you are keen on growing as an investor. But you must be careful with the contracts you settle for as not all sales are as profitable as they look.

Sometimes the value of five deals may be in one, and your responsibility is to search for that one in a thousand that will boost your investment portfolio and add value to your investment process.

We will begin with the first objective of this chapter and then proceed to finalize the second objective.

How to Get Real Estate Deals

Below, you will find a lot of options that will be instrumental in helping you find an excellent real estate deal. Now you can either use all suggestions below or try out a few (it all depends on you and your time).

There are multiple ways to secure a good deal, try the approaches, and then be smart enough to know what will work and what won't add any value.

Take a drive around

When you have the time, go for a ride around the neighborhood and search for properties you may want to purchase.

So what are you looking for as you drive?

Search for vacant properties; these are properties with a stuffed mailbox, a bad roof, poorly kept lawn and other signs showing you that no one lives there or the landlord doesn't care for the property anymore.

As you make stops, take notes about each property that catches your eye and the details, and you can snap a photo to remember the building. When you get back home, research each of the houses.

Search for the owner through public records, write a letter stating your offer to the owner or send a mail. Driving around the neighborhood is a cost-effective way of securing deals.

You wouldn't need agents, and you get to see the property for what it is instead of pictures that may be misleading. You also get a personalized assessment of the area.

This step toward finding deals will enable you to make well-grounded decisions about your real estate investment. Also, look out for houses that are for sale by owner. These can often be good deals because the seller doesn't have to give a commission to a real estate agent.

Spread the Word

Another great way of finding deals is by spreading the word and telling people what you need. We take this step for granted because we assume that people wouldn't respond.

But who else will know better when there is a deal than people? Real estate deals fall through every minute of every day, and these are transactions enabled by people.

By spreading the word, those you tell who have sold properties in the past will know about your offer, and the next time they have a property for sale or know someone with a property for sale they will reach out to you.

You will become successful with your business based on the extent of passion you exhibit. If you are passionate about real estate investment, you will talk about it to everyone.

You'll most likely be in many social situations that will give you the opportunity to talk about your investment interests with others. Be sure to put out feelers that you're interested in vacant properties. Word of mouth can be a lucrative way to find out about properties for sale, especially those that have yet to be advertised by a Realtor and those who are for sale by owner.

Use the MLS (Multiple Listing Service)

MLS is still a common way to find properties; it is an abbreviation for Multiple Listing Services, which is also a collection of systems and services that stores information about homes for sale.

To get the best result with MLS, you will have to work closely with a real estate agent or real estate company that has access to the MLS database.

When you search on other real estate websites for deals, you are mostly getting information from MLS, and there is a way to use this pool of properties for the good of your investment plans.

First, ensure that you are fast with your offers; the potential buyer who offers a good price will most likely get a "Yes." Be the early bird who gets the best out of sales, and there are some things you can do to increase your speed with making offers.

Ensure that you know what you want to buy so you don't have to go through the process of sorting through all listings. Instead of focusing on the 99 percent of deals, try to focus on the one percent you need.

Also, you can create automatic alerts that enable you to see properties as soon as they are listed.

Another way to be among the first to be notified of income property for sale is to ask a real estate agent to send you alerts.

These alerts will be emailed to you as soon as the listing is prepared to go live. You'll be among the first to tour the property if you so please.

Aside from being the first to make an offer, you can get more out of MLS by being the last to make an offer, this way you can buy at a cheaper rate if the property is still available. A more significant percentage of sellers will surely reduce their initial asking price if they were unable to make a sale after the first six months.

You need to tell the agent you are working with to give you a list of properties that have been on the market for over six months and start making offers on them. You will get a good deal at a good price.

However, the problem with MLS is this; everyone is using it because it is a large pool of the bestselling properties. So using this method is akin to searching where everyone else is looking.

But you can still use MLS to get the right deals; you need to put in the work and remain dedicated to the process. Making an effort with real estate is better than not doing anything at all.

Direct Mail

Direct mail entails sending out a large number of targeted letters to people who may be interested in selling their properties. Direct mail marketers assure real estate investors that this process works, but you will need to be very patient.

If you send out maybe 100 letters, there is a considerable chance that you will get about 30 phone calls with people wanting more information. Out of the 30 who called, you would most likely get about five real deals but then settle for the best two.

Direct mail serves dual purposes, aside from being a source for getting deals, it can also provide you with raw data on what is in the marketplace.

For example, out of the 30 prospects who called if 20 of them say that they have similar properties up for sale in the market, it should let you know that that there is a better chance at closing a deal at a cheaper rate with any one of them.

You may be wondering why anyone would sell their property to an investor who sent mail. Well, some people wouldn't want to sell through a real estate agent because they want to avoid paying the commission. When they sell directly to you, they get to keep all of the proceeds.

The people who buy through direct mail may also be faced with a nasty divorce and want to sell off the property swiftly. It could be someone in a foreclosure battle and might lose his home.

Direct mail enables people to find solutions to their real estate problems. You will be right there to resolve it for them while getting an excellent deal.

The success of direct mail is in the power of repetition and consistency, hence the reason you will require patience. So send out those emails regularly—at least monthly.

It is all about when opportunity presents itself, so someday one of the recipients of your mail may want to sell a property or will know someone who wants to sell. You will be the first investor to be contacted because you have been consistent with your mails.

Eviction Courts/Records

The deals you seek might be in your local courthouse. Evictions from a landlord's point of view are stressful, tiring, and with a hefty bill when it all ends.

Some landlords would instead give up the property entirely than go through the pain of an eviction; hence, the reason real estate investors need to target landlords on the verge of eviction.

These landlords deal with a problem, and the problem is a motivating factor for them to get rid of the property; this is where you become essential. But how do you know the landlords who are about to evict tenants?

You find that information in public records. Evictions are a part of public records in a lot of countries. You need to take a trip down to the local county administration office to get a list of recent evictions.

The ways through which you can get the list varies from state to state so if you are unsure, make inquiries at the county office or the courts. You can get this information from court records as well.

After getting the list, use the information it contains to ascertain if the properties suit your investment goals, if yes go ahead and call the landlord. Now you need to be sure that the deal you make with the landlord is just right considering the state of the property. The landlord may be desperate to sell; the question is, are you desperate to buy?

As a side note: Some newspapers publish foreclosure and eviction records if a judgment has been placed against the tenant. Some municipalities post the information on their websites.

Craigslist

Craigslist is a bulletin-style platform for posting ads, sharing information and buying/selling items. Although the platform isn't solely for real estate, you can get deals because agents share listings with the audience to get buyers.

You can access Craigslist to peruse and seek properties that are for sale. Aside from looking through the ads posted by others, you can also post your ad on Craigslist.

You never know who may be seeking a buyer, so post an ad

saying you buy properties. Make sure your ad is in a particular way such that it captures what you seek.

If your ad is not specific enough, you might get offers that do not match your expectations. Reading through all offers is a waste of time. Another easy way to use Craigslist in your search for deals is to contact landlords.

Most landlords are barely enjoying the proceeds of their properties. They cannot make a sale because they feel like the property will not fetch them a reasonable sum of money. Some of these landlords could be older people, and if their property suits what you need, you just might a good deal.

Call the landlords, explain what you need, tell them you are looking to invest in real estate, you saw their post, and you are interested. Some landlords may reply stating that they don't want to sell and they only want to rent.

Don't worry if they refuse to sell; they may have some other deal for you by referring you to someone else. You can also build a business relationship with landlords from Craigslist such that whenever they have information on contracts, they will reach out to you.

Online Marketplace

Is there anything you cannot get online today? If you think about it, you will agree that the online space is where you should be searching for deals.

Everyone is online!

The person who will offer you a fantastic deal is online, they posting and sharing. There is a belief that if you are selling anything online, you will surely get a buyer.

Start with social media and use the platforms intentionally to seek deals. There are a lot of real estate influencers on social media sites such as Instagram, Facebook, or Twitter.

When you follow such influencers, you will always have information on deals. You won't need to go through the influencers who made the post when you are ready to buy; contact the seller and take it from there.

If you have a specific area or city in mind, use the location feature online to find those who regularly post about properties. Gain insight into what happens in the real estate scene in such markets.

You can also pitch your sales ideas easily when you see a deal you want online right on the platform and hopefully make a sale.

Do you recall in chapter one we recommended blogs as a way of getting real estate investment education? While learning from such a blog, you can search for deals.

Some bloggers make money by posting available properties on their blogs. You might not get the perfect deal you seek with the first post, but if you continue searching, you might find it.

On the online market space, you can post ads, use your personal social media platforms to share what you need in properties and see what happens.

Property Management Companies

Management companies have access to places in a city that offers the best deals to investors. Such companies know the ins and outs of suburbs, street layouts, neighborhoods, office spaces, etc.

When a deal is about to pull through, they are usually one of the first to know and having a good relationship with them can help you secure good sales.

Some sellers trust property management companies, hence the reason they go to them when they want to make a sale. The sellers will also listen to the company's advice on the choice of buyer

You will need to reach out to a good property management company, strike up a relationship and ensure that they give you full access to the kind of deals you seek. In some cases, you might have to pay a fee to get this kind of service

If you pay, it will be worthwhile because you will be getting regular deal briefs that are solid leads. Take the relationship with the company further by getting them to send deals on properties that are in bad shape.

If you have the capital to invest in improvements for some properties, then you must know that after the renovations the value of the property will increase and you get to earn more.

Some properties already have the potential for high sales, but because the previous tenants didn't maintain it well enough, it lost value.

Deals on properties to be renovated and put back on the market are always the right way of making more money from your sales or rent. Make sure you have the money for renovations before accepting the deal.

Networking

A lot of successful investors have gotten amazing deals just by being a part of a network of other successful investors or people who are interested in properties.

As a beginner, gain a lot of value by joining high-level networks. With such systems, you do not only get ideas on how to get better but also get authentic and profitable deals.

An excellent example of such networks could be an association of landlords or a group of commercial brokers. For some of these groups, there are no stringent conditions in place for you to become a member.

Before becoming an investor, you didn't know about the

existence of such groups. But now that you are taking the investor pathway, you shouldn't only know about them; you should join them.

For some of these networks, there is a free flow of information and deals. You can learn a whole lot in one meeting than you would when you try to get deals online or on your own.

If you don't access to deals directly from your network, you can also gain insight into the best places to search. Think of real estate networks as a group of people with common interests.

When people have common goals, their conversations will be about their goals, and if you listen (and contribute) to their conversational discourses will gain a lot.

In some cases, an investor in such meetings might have information on an off-market deal but doesn't have the resources to secure it. The investor might be willing to talk to you about it, thus giving you access to an off-market deal with little or no competitive offers.

You will also be networking with landlords who are willing to make a sale but need a good offer. Don't trivialize the importance of networking as an investor, especially concerning getting deals.

Real estate clubs also exist in some neighborhoods, but you've got to find such clubs and let people know what you are seeking to buy.

How to know you've Found A Great Deal

You know where to find deals now! But how do you ascertain if you've found a great property? You already have the assurance of getting a lot of good leads from the tips above, but the truth is that you must narrow down all your points to that one valuable deal.

The steps you will find below will empower you to align your search with your goals as an investor. You can get deals that are not only good on paper but great choices for your investment.

The area is consistently improving

Regardless of your investment objectives (you will learn more about this shortly), you cannot accept a deal with properties in bad neighborhoods with no sign of hope.

Impoverished areas attract problematic tenants who will cause your property to go down in value, making it impossible for you to sell it later. So when you get all of these great leads and deals, find out if the area already improves consistently.

If you don't want to wait until you get a deal to figure this out, then go out and look for those areas intentionally. Here is a tip, follow Starbucks! Every new location for Starbucks is a potentially improved area.

In a Starbuck area, you will notice that people are renovating homes. The government is investing in parks and roads, yards are getting cleaned up, and more developers are purchasing land.

The Starbucks trick also works because the company will not open new outlets in areas they know holds no promise for their business. What can you learn from Starbucks as an investor?

The lesson from the company is simple, invest in places you are sure of returns. Monitor the area and see if it matches the investment ideas you've got. Starbucks knows their ideal customer and those that can afford their products, so they take the product to those people by setting up outlets in their neighborhood.

As a real estate investor, you should think in that light by ensuring that the deal you settle for represents a property in a consistently improving environment.

There is a caveat, though, the fact that the area is improving doesn't mean you will make money off buying property there instantly. To ensure faster sales, you will have to research the vacancy rates of the area, population changes, and the economic value of the place.

You found a growing market

After ascertaining the improvement of the area, you need to check that the market where the deal originates is a growing one.

Before committing to the agreement, before signing on the dotted lines, make sure the property is in an increasing market.

A growing market is an area with highly sought after properties. In some countries, an example of an increasing demand could be the capital cities where there is always an influx of people who are willing to buy, lease or rent a property.

In such a market, you wouldn't be stuck with a deal because it will only be a matter of time before you get clients swarming over your property. This growth is the reason for the initial advice offered to you, don't be thrilled by having so many leads.

Be concerned about the compatibility of the deal with your desire for consistent income generation. Of course, every transaction cannot be from a growing market; in fact, the sales from such markets are harder to come by than others.

But the truth is, if you are patient enough in your search from deals out of the hundreds of options you get, you might get the one that matters most. That one deal will also enable you to get firm footing as an investor.

A property in a growing market has over a 20 percent profit appreciation rate because the market is consistent with growth. Such places appeal to people even more because there is an attraction.

Growing markets are places for upward social mobility, networking with the elites, and the right business place for aggressive businesses who seek better clientele.

So regardless of the kind of property you will be getting (homes or offices), there is a vast potential for investment growth.

The deal meets your long-term investment objectives

Before you start investing, you need to set goals and objectives. When writing an exam, you will need to aim for a particular score, and this score inspired your reading pattern and the dedication you put into excelling at the course.

For you to identify a deal that is great for you, you need to have investment goals and then watch if a deal matches your goals. You need to ask if the agreement will help you bring your goals to fruition else it wouldn't be valuable.

For example, if you set your objective at earning $500 per month in cash flow, you need a deal that will help you get that money. However, it is easier to get this kind of cash flow from multi-unit properties. Examples of such features include duplexes, an apartment building with about 3-4 units of a basement suite.

When you find this kind of property, use the Gross Rent Multiplier to calculate what you would be getting. Get your asking price, monthly rent and then multiply the monthly rent by 12 (yearly income).

The thread doesn't end with finding a good deal but checking to ensure that the agreement aligns with your investment objectives and goals.

The most exciting aspect of being a real estate investor isn't getting the right property (as opposed to popular opinion). The thrill is in the search for deals, and it is this way because the process of the search will expose you to first-hand information about how the market works.

When you search for deals, you become an experienced investor who doesn't only have general information on the state of the market. You will have real-time lessons from the streets, make mistakes, pull yourself back up and win through the search.

But for most of these deals to fall through, you will need money. So what happens when you don't have money? Can a real estate investor still make some progress with investment even without cash? You will discover the answers in the next chapter.

Chapter Five: How to Invest in Real Estate without MONEY!

This title of this chapter must have gotten your attention right from the table of contents as you wonder how it is possible to invest without spending money. Well, you are about to get answers. This chapter will empower you to unearth some fantastic investment opportunities that don't require you using your money.

Are you ready to learn?

OPM (Other people's money)

Use other people's money to invest in a property!

The first idea you should realize about this step is the fact that there is money everywhere! Completed transactions happen every minute, and people do them with money they want to invest but don't have the time to search for a good deal.

You know where the good deals are so this is where you become valuable. You've received a whole lecture on finding good deals from the beginning of this book to this point, but you don't have money.

So you are a connecting bridge between a person's desire to invest and a good investment option. You will also earn from the process without any of your money.

If you can get a 20 percent ROI on a property, then you can get someone else who has $100,000 sitting in the bank waiting for an investment opportunity. You can use that money to invest in the property.

So where will you get someone to trust you with their money for real estate investment? Well, start with friends and family; these are people who know and trust you.

Within your inner circle, some people have money in their bank account for investment purposes–pitch your idea to them.

Borrow their money to buy the property and give them a fixed return of about five or 10 percent of the investment on their money. The percentage you offer is better than what you will get from any bank, and guess what? You can keep the extra funds.

So you just invested and made a profit without contributing a cent of your money. This step is different from a joint venture because in a joint venture, the parties have stakes in the property.

With this idea, you are entirely in charge, once you pay back the fixed amount from the proceeds of the investment, you will be fine. It doesn't always have to be your money.

Another way of using other people's money is by getting a bank loan to put down and buy a property. If the property in question is valuable and can get you the kind of ROI you expect to pay the bank, you will get a loan quickly.

Banks are after one thing—maximizing their funds. If a person goes to the bank, saying "Give me money, I will buy this property, and within a few years you will get your money back with interest," the bank will surely cooperate!

First, you need to make sure you've done the research, and you are confident of the property's potential before approaching the bank. Banks only care about numbers, show them good numbers, and you've got their attention.

Joint Venture

With a joint venture you work with someone else, it is a situation where you and this other person bring in 50 percent of the value to strike a deal. If the venture of choice is property, then the VALUE has to be equal because it's a partnership.

Here is where it gets interesting:

Your 50 percent value doesn't have to be money. Your contribution could be something else, such as property expertise. So your partner brings the other 50 percent value, which is the money needed to finance the investment.

Your partner is the financier of the project while you take on the role of implementing the plan.

With the partnership, you use the knowledge gained from materials such as this book to find the right deals. So your partner is confident about the investment.

You are bringing 50 percent of your knowledge, property instincts, managerial skills at overseeing the property, vetting tenants, etc. This idea of investing in real estate without your money helps you understand how the world works: that money is not the sole entity in an investment plan.

When you show your joint venture partner figures and projections of the deal, they will be unwilling to go on without you. Yes, your partner has the money, but what good is cash without investment?

Your partner puts the money in, you put in the time and energy to make it work and you both split the ROI equally. This way, you have just bought a property without your money. It feels good repeating this idea because sometimes it seems unbelievable, but it is possible, and it has to sink into your investor mindset.

But when going into a joint venture with another person, you must be careful. First, you and your partner must have precise expectations. Know what the brain box of the deal and your partner needs to have the money ready when it is time.

More importantly, you must have a contract with the details of the agreement. Do not rely on VERBAL CONTRACT (it is a huge mistake).

Even if your venture partner is your best friend or family member, insist on a contract that clearly states what you both are bringing to the table. We don't anticipate a conflict of interest, but we must prepare for them. (A smart investor is always prepared.)

Seller/Owner Financing

Owner financing is a financing arrangement that entails the seller allowing the buyer to make payments in installments. The buyer (you) doesn't need to get a loan from the bank. Owner financing is a vital tool that provides an opportunity for you and the seller to earn.

With this agreement, you completely bypass the bank and deal directly with the seller, pay in installments until you pay off the price of the property, and it's yours.

This process is without your money, which is why anyone who desires to invest in real estate can use seller/owner financing. When you get access to the property, lease it, and pay the owner from the profit you make.

For example, if you found a seller with a property worth $50,000 and you cannot go to the bank to get a loan, and you don't have the cash. You can offer the seller financing option to the seller and promise to pay the $50,000 over a specified period.

The deal will also include interest for several years (maybe 10-20) years, which will cause the seller to become interested in the offer. But, as always, like the smart investor that you are, you must make sure you are utilizing the right property.

Of course, the tides in the market may change. But remember that properties appreciate over time, so if you are strategic with your choice of property you might have a significant investment deal on your hands.

Owner financing is a cheaper and faster way of closing a real estate deal that is beneficial to both sellers and buyers. Be prepared to convince the seller to get on board.

Some relevant documents you will need while finalizing your deal with the seller are *promissory notes* which stimulates your promise to fulfill the details of the agreement.

In the documents, you will find the amount of the property, terms of repayment, interest rate, the repayment schedule, and how payments are made (quarterly, monthly, etc.). Promissory notes also contain the type of penalties for late payment with the terms and conditions for early payoffs.

If you stick to the agreement, and you are smart with your choice of property, you will enjoy the benefits of owner financing. You will be getting monthly revenues from rent without paying upfront for the property.

You will also have a robust deal with the seller while bypassing the bank all without using personal funds.

Lease Option Agreement

With a lease option agreement, you can get a property today, generate income from it through rent with the RIGHT (not an obligation) to buy it later, which is akin to the owner of the property giving you a free loan for several years (maybe five, seven years, etc.).

The only money you pay with this agreement is the solicitor fee, and you get access to the property for the agreed time frame without spending a dime for the property itself. You will be getting immediate cash flow with the property by renting it out. But here is the biggest shocker, your capital appreciates as the house goes up in value.

Properties increase in value all the time; this persistent increase in value is one of the hallmarks of real estate investment (appreciation). So by the time you are ready to pay for the property: maybe ten years later you will find that the property has increased in value such that you can pay the seller and still have some ROI with the property as your own!

On top of all benefits in ten or five years, you gain an increase in income through monthly cash flow from rent because you own the property.

With the monies that come in monthly, you can diversify into other viable investment options that also help you generate more income, quite extreme right?

With a lease option agreement, you can own more than one property without spending your money while earning from all the houses.

There are two separate agreements in one lease option agreement:

- You and the landlord can agree on a monthly payment plan, which entails you managing the property, renting it to tenants for-profit and paying a part of it to the landlord.

- You can agree on a price, how much you will buy the property later (if you wish to.

The lease option agreement is a fantastic way to start investing without any money or even if you can't get a mortgage. If you have been reading from the start of this book to this point and you were worried about getting money to invest well, here you have it: you don't need money!

You may wonder, how do I get someone who owns a property to agree to a lease option agreement? You need to seek out motivated sellers who want to give up these properties because of the challenges they deal with while holding on to the property.

You are looking for tired landlords, people dealing with nasty divorce cases and other people who see the property as a burden. That burden becomes a real estate asset to you that can help you jumpstart your investment career.

There are thousands of people who have become rich using this agreement, so this idea isn't a novel one in the market. The problem is that very few people take the leap and the few who do courageously earn massively.

Every enjoyable journey comes to an end, and we have reached the end of ours, but unlike other trips, ours will create a ripple effect into your future. Everything you've learned thus far will have more meaning as you implement and put them to action.

So we have one more section to go, and you can start the process of being a real estate investor. The next chapter will inspire you to SUSTAIN all of this gained knowledge long-term.

Please Note: Most of the ideas shared in this chapter require a lot of thought and expertise to execute it flawlessly. Before utilizing any of the steps, make sure you have all the bases covered. Carry out proper research about the choice of property and its propensity for increased value.

Tax Lien Investments

Tax Lien investments are a way to buy property with little cash outlay, however, it does come with risks.

Tax liens become available when a property owner falls behind in paying their property tax. It generally must be behind several years. At that time, some municipalities hope to recoup their losses by selling tax liens. The buyer doesn't actually own the property at the time of the sale, but they hold the lien.

The purchaser of the lien can eventually own the property after a certain amount of time by foreclosure. The waiting period varies from county to county.

Illinois is a large tax lien state and holds auctions frequently. They offer online catalogs for out-of-town investors to view the available properties.

The properties should be examined carefully as some may be in unsatisfactory areas and some houses might be in poor condition and repairs would cost more than the property is worth.

Some offerings are vacant land, hence it's a good idea to check with the municipality for allowed uses. If it's vacant farmland, ask if there are agricultural tax exemptions available.

If you can't or don't want to attend a property lien auction, there are companies who will do the bidding for you. They will purchase the properties in your name and change you a nominal fee.

The owner can redeem the property at any time by paying the lien. There is a risk to all tax lien investing, however, it can be a profitable venture for those willing to take a gamble.

There's plenty of information about tax lien investing on the internet. It is a complex subject and rather than get into every detail of it in this book, it's best you do your own research and talk to those who have had successful investments.

Some states handle defaulted properties by holding auctions by which the buyer owns the property outright once the bidding price has been paid.

When an owner defaults on tax payments for several years, the municipality takes deed to the property. It is then offered at an auction, generally held once a year. These auctions are often held on site and online. In other words, electronic bidding is accepted at the time of the auction.

The minimum bid is the cost of the back taxes. These properties are most often in decent shape.

As with any foreclosure, sometimes the evicted owner will damage the property by punching holes in the walls, flooding by leaving a bathtub or sink running, or turning off the heat when it's freezing outside, causing a pipe to burst resulting in massive water damage.

Vacant land is a most often a good deal because there's not a lot of damage done to parcels.

A new and increasingly popular means of disposing of foreclosed or abandoned property is through what's called land banks. Land banks are controlled by local governments, usually a local government with a county government.

Land banks serve to renovate or demolish existing structures, depending on the condition, and resell to investors willing to invest in the community.

This leads to a side note that was mentioned earlier. It would behoove you to look into any grants available for distressed property renovation. Some communities offer such grants in an effort to clean up a certain neighborhood. This gives the real estate investor an opportunity to own a property for little to no cost and rent to respectable tenants. The ROI can be excellent.

Stay in touch with your local government to learn of these opportunities. Most have community development offices, and you can ask to be placed on their mailing list. Their websites are good sources if they keep them up to date. Sadly, some don't but it doesn't take a lot of time to check.

Chapter Six: The Concept of Sustaining Your Investment Long-Term

It's the end of a fantastic journey, and you will agree that it has been the most exciting read. We started with the basics of real estate investment then gradually built on a lot of other fundamental concepts.

What you have received thus far is a comprehensive guide on how to become a real estate investor. If you implement everything you've read and the ideas you've received, you are sure of attaining success with your investment.

So what does this last chapter entail?

There is a pattern of learning that is common these days; it entails people learning to forget! They learn new and productive things, practice for a few weeks and don't maintain the consistency.

The inability for most learners to sustain what they learn is because they don't know HOW to implement sustainability. Every other book and the online courses teach them how to do what they want to do but not how to create a successful pattern with the ideas.

Now you have learned how to become an investor. Just like so many other people, but what distinguishes you from them is the power you gained with information on how you can *remain* a successful investor.

When I was putting this book together, I thought about you! The reader who is probably reading his/her first intensive book on real estate investment.

You who experienced investing for a short while. The person who gave up too quickly because of a lack of proper preparedness and fear.

I thought about the individual who has the potential to be a great investor but doesn't know what to do or the next step to take. You were at the focal point of every research and information that was gathered to curate this book.

But, more importantly, the information isn't meant to enable you to be an average investor. An average investor buys properties at will, sells or rents when he feels like and swims with the tide.

This book is for the PHENOMENAL INVESTOR who not only kick-starts the investment process but also uses the details in this book to create a lasting legacy.

For you to achieve legacy, you must build sustainability, which also equates to staying power and the ability to remain at the top of the sector with disruptive and futuristic investment deals.

We will round off this experience in a compelling way that will prompt you to take and sustain actionable steps, ready?

How to Sustain Investments Long-Term

Stay Educated

Learning never ends!

We started with this idea in chapter one, and we are back to it because education is a powerful tool, even for investors. Unlike when you started reading this book, you know so much already and that is when the challenge strikes.

You start to feel like you know everything. You have read enough, and now you are investing in the market, so what more information could you learn?

Most unsuccessful investors lose out in the market because from the moment they started investing, they also stopped learning. Now they are in this ever-evolving sector with stale information and cannot seem to make better decisions based on new realities.

Unlike when you were a beginner, now you need advanced learning, so take on more advanced real estate courses. Register for high-powered conferences with experienced speakers and seasoned investors.

It was okay for you to attend free seminars and get free eBooks as a beginner, but now you are beyond that. When building sustainability, you will spend money on investor education. The inspiration you need for the next big decision will not be in the pages of regular blogs and free books.

When you invest in exceptional education, you will surely have good rewards and results to show for your commitment to learning.

Diversify your ROI

There is danger in a single market!

Now you have started earning from your investments, and it seems like you are having a great time enough to not think about further investment options.

Great investors know that with the real estate market despite consistent property appreciation, there can be drastic changes. What will you do when suddenly you don't have suitable tenants for your property or when investment seems like a drag?

If you don't diversify, you will lose the spark and excitement that comes with investing, solution? Use what you get as ROI from your existing investments to fund other investment ideas!

Even now, as a beginner, you can start research on some other viable investment options you can try out while still in the real estate game.

If you want to be excellent and remain financially stable, you cannot stick to a single investment platform. There is so much beauty in experiencing these diverse investment opportunities;

you get to have a diversified and robust portfolio that helps you earn passive income for life.

Sustainability is not strictly about maintaining a particular stance; it is about building yourself up so you can do better than your past. A diversified portfolio will surely give you an edge any day and anywhere.

You will also become very knowledgeable experientially because you will be delving into different sectors and markets. An investor never stops; he/she seeks ways to use funds for multiplied impact. Even if you are not inclined to build a diverse portfolio right now, as you continue, you will find that your interest increases.

With diversification, you also reduce investment risks by allocating funds to industries, financial instruments, and other categories. The process of diversifying your portfolio will enable you to maximize returns from different areas that react to the same event.

Put you avoid putting all your eggs in one basket!

Recession is a national event that affects every aspect of a country's economy. If you had a single investment option plan in your portfolio (real estate), at the time of the recession, you would be in a dilemma.

However, if you have investments in start-ups, blue-chip companies, etc. you will not feel the impact of the recession as severely as you would with a single investment plan.

The location also matters when considering diversification!

So think beyond your geographical location as volatility with stocks in the United States might not be the same in China. By taking your investments beyond the borders of your region, you will be minimizing risks.

Be Conscious of Market Trends

Listen to what the market is saying!

When you are a real estate investor, you need to listen to a lot of things (people inclusive) but above all of the ideas and people, listen to the market. You need to pay close attention to the market trends because it is only through the patterns you can gain information on happenings in the market at a particular time.

If you invest in stocks, a stockbroker will advise that you pay attention to the stock market and the fluctuations in the market. When you take your focus off the market for a few days, you may come back to crashed stocks, plummeted price and any other surprise.

Sometimes what you need to make your next move is in the market trend. You only need to monitor it long enough to be able to predict how it moves.

There are periods when people only rent office spaces. You will notice that most of your fellow investors have new tenants who are business owners. If all of these happens consecutively within a particular month, then it's a sign.

What this trend means is that if you strategize well enough, you can buy a property and develop it before that month, put it on the market and cash out on office rentals.

What about during festive seasons? Are people spending more on rented properties for a few weeks when they travel into your area? You can set a separate investment fund aside for properties to acquire for that purpose.

When you follow market trends, you also find properties to buy at a lower rate because the pattern will highlight properties not being sold. So you can buy such properties below market price.

When the market trend turns again to highlight the relevance of that property you bought at a cheaper rate, rent will not be the sole option for a massive ROI. Once you put it on the market for sale at an increased rate, you will get a buyer.

Be Resilient

A resilient person inspires others!

Being a real estate investor who can hold his/her own for years is quite admirable, but it requires a lot of resilience. For you to consistently inspire yourself and others, you must be committed to the process of investment. Being resilient means, you don't buy a property today, and the next time you consider repurchasing one is ten years later. So much can happen in ten years, and if you lack resilience, you will no longer be relevant as an investor.

When you listen to older men and women who have been investing for years and have written books, now mentoring others, what do you hear in their voices?

If you listen well, you will hear traces of commitment and resilience through so many years of being active in the market. So determination is crucial in both excellent and tumultuous times.

There will be times when the market experiences a shake-up, and people are afraid to buy properties because they are worried about value and appreciation.

So such persons stay away from investing until it becomes conducive for them again. In high times they are investors, but in uncertain times they are regular folks.

I don't think you've come from the beginning of this book until this point to be regular. You didn't commit yourself to read and implementing to be like everyone else.

Be resilient at all times!

You must be a courageous and bold investor else you will be swept away by the tides of challenges. Building resilience should be at this beginning stage of your journey, make up your mind that no matter what you wouldn't give up,

With your heart set on being resilient, you will mentally remain poised for the investment ride with so much excitement and optimism.

Discover Why You Failed

Failure is the best teacher!

If you are going to sustain your investment pathway long-term, you will have to think about failure differently. There are stories from investors who say that they never attempted to invest in a particular area or city because they tried multiple times in the past and failed at it.

So in their own words, they are playing it "safe" by avoiding situations that will make them fail and stick to proven successful trends. But investors who play it safe never become incredibly successful, they can make a few monies here and there, but it ends there.

Instead of shying away from failure, LEARN FROM IT!

The statement "Seek the silver lining in the cloud" applies to this step. There is a silver lining in that mistake you made; you don't know it yet because you are focused on the wrong picture.

Stop looking at what went wrong, start asking why it went wrong. When you discover that you've made a mistake with a deal, instead of throwing pity parties, go back to the drawing table.

At the drawing table, realistically assess the situation if possible, from a third party's perspective. What could you have done better? Did you check all the boxes before committing to the deal? What about the property itself? Was the property good enough?

If you quickly move on after a bad deal, you will most likely make the same mistake next time, and that's how an unproductive circle starts. But you can prevent the ring entirely by being positive about failure.

Always unravel the process of every transaction even after the negative experience so you can prevent further mishaps in the future. Investors learn from themselves occasionally, but the best teachers you will have while investing are your mistakes and failures.

Experiment with New Markets

There is always something new to explore!

We are going to discuss the value of having a specific niche soon. Before we get to that step, you should know that there is value in having an open mind toward new markets.

Oftentimes, we read about other investors investing in new markets, how they had losses, and this gives us cold feet. But on the flip side, some people take the plunge and then become the pioneers of such new markets, cashing in early and cementing their place as principal founders.

First, become aware of emerging markets, and this can only happen when you are proactive with acquiring knowledge. I am not talking about basic knowledge out there but going beyond the surface.

When you're always amid great thinking investors, you will get the most unusual yet disruptive ideas for investing, which may be the future of the market. So this explains the keyword "Experiment."

New markets here do not solely refer to new opportunities within your neighborhood or country. We are thinking globally at this point, and global new markets are emerging daily all over the world.

Being able to identify with these new markets is one of the hallmarks of a good investor. In sharing ideas on sustainability, you need to know that there is much more out there.

You don't have to start by traveling to an African country because you read about an opportunity for investors. You can begin by first getting an education on how to identify potentially successful new markets that are beyond your immediate reach.

Get books, research online, ask questions within your network, and actively seek out these markets. When you get ideas, vet them and then experiment with little money first.

These are new sectors in areas you are not familiar with, so it isn't advisable to put a whole lot of money all at once into investing. Find someone who loves the idea of new markets to be your collaborator. Then if there is a more significant percentage of investment opportunity, invest in a few units at first.

If it works as you anticipated, you could do more units and continue to expand your interest. If it doesn't work out, learn your lessons from that market and seek other opportunities.

Regardless of the positive or negative results, don't stop for anything, keep on moving!

Build a Stronger Team

Go faster with others!

At the beginning of your investment experience, you may be more inclined to do almost everything yourself. Wanting to do it all is not because you don't need help but because you cannot afford to hire people.

As you advance with investments, you will need to build a strong team. As a beginner, you have fewer goals that may entail, buying a property, renting it, and earning ROI.

After a few years, you will be aiming for the more prominent deals which include buying multiple properties at once, while renting and selling as you develop them.

You will need to team to make this bigger dream come to fruition. So you will need an attorney, a real estate agent, a licensed inspector and anyone else that will add value to your vestment process

Another reason for a team is because as you get better at investing, you will want to expand your reach. Expansion can be by purchasing properties across state lines or even in other countries.

So are you going to be at every property deal within and outside the country? With a team, you can be in different places at the same time. You can add more investment options to your portfolio, and you can win with every deal.

Ensure that you have the right people on your team. The people you should connect with are those who appreciate the value of vision. Get in contact with those willing to build with you. Don't settle for team members that are motivated only by money!

Understand Risks

Know how risks work; don't fear them!

If you asked people who are not real estate investors to mention a reason for their hesitation, "risk" will be at the top of the results.

Everyone wants to make money, but no one wants to take risks. As an investor for you to avoid the pitfall of quitting at the start of your investment, you must understand risks.

Every investment opportunity has its risk level; there is a risk of investing in education. Risks mean investing in the stock market or start-ups; there is no investment option without risks.

Yet, there are millions of people making a ton of profit from these "Risky" ventures. The difference between the investor who is cashing in and the one who isn't is understanding risks.

The real estate billionaires in the world are not intimidated by risks (regardless of its magnitude). Instead, they take their time to study the risk factors. Learn how it applies to each sector of the market, and they used what they unearth to make informed decisions.

When you understand risks, you then start to take "calculated" ones with an awareness that it is risky but worth it in the end. Don't run away from risky ventures; the one percent wealthiest people in the world thrive on risks.

Such persons do not back down and would continually persist until they succeed. Yes, it may sound very motivational right now, but you need to hear this as you make your entry into the market.

You can manage risks, and they can be a source of inspiration for you. Managing and understanding risks are some of the reasons why you need a reliable team. You might feel overwhelmed going through property briefs and analyzing risk factors.

But with a team, you will have access to multiple opinions and insight into the best way to handle a project that seems risky. When next you get an uncertain deal, don't back down. See beyond the risk by gaining understanding and then plan; you will either win or learn a lesson (which is crucial for your investment experience).

Utilize the Power of a Network

You are as successful as your network!

The point is so important: you are one investor, but you need others to succeed as well, and that is where a robust network becomes crucial.

Remember that as an investor, you are a businessman/woman, and one of the best rules of business all over the world is that collaboration makes you move faster.

Within your country, state, city, or local community, there are several other real estate investors, reach out to them! How else will you know the best and hottest areas to invest based on experience? How will you obtain information about how you can get loans quickly?

How will you know about desperate landlords who are interested in lease option agreement? Your network can help you take the right action at the right time just by feeding you with the right set of information.

As a beginner, access to networks right now may be strict but don't remain like that. You are the one who needs the system; you are the one who needs to grow capacity so you must seek out such successful individuals.

If there is a real estate investor club in your neighborhood, sign up to join. If there is an investor you've always admired, send an email, and try to have a meeting.

Networks do not happen without effort. Until you start building your system now, you will be a lone ranger who is isolated from the pack of wolves.

Most of the time, you will need a network because of deals. As within real estate investors' events, some investors have great deals but cannot execute them due to certain constraints. Now if you are in the right circle of investors and you can implement such transactions, it will be given to you.

The investors who try to do things alone always struggle while others dwell in abundance. Such investors are the ones who dissuade others from investing in real estate because nothing is inspiring about their story.

But when you meet investors with high-end and influential networks, you will notice that they are always willing to help. They have a track record of successful transactions on display.

You can build both online and offline networks. Online networks are formed by joining real estate groups on social media and connecting with other investors online.

Search for websites dedicated to real estate investors (doesn't have to be a site in your country), join real estate communities on platforms such as Facebook and get interactive with other investors.

One thing is sure with having an investor network; you will always have numerous platforms and opportunities to learn. As you already know, learning is everything with investment.

Be Intentional With Everything

A calculative investor is a smart one!

Know what you want or what you are looking for and go for it; that is what it means to be an intentional investor. A lack of intentionality implies the presence of uncertainty, and that is not a trait any real estate investor should exhibit.

In chapter four, you were encouraged to set property goals because that is what intentional and calculative investors do. The word "spontaneity" doesn't have much value in the real estate world because you are dealing with money.

So you cannot afford to be less than intentional with anything. Buy properties intentionally, rent or sell deliberately, don't take chances with the investment process and not on what someone else is doing or someone else's method.

If you are going to be in this game for the long haul, you will have to develop an adamant mind. A mindset that enables you to make a confident decision regardless of what is "popular."

Intentional people get the most out of life, even when they sometimes seem too "slow" for others. But one move from them is worth more than five quick steps from other investors.

When you are intentional, you hardly make mistakes, and even when you do, it is easier to bounce back quickly. Take the time to think through a deal and then go for it because YOU WANT TO!

Purchase Facts, Not Emotions

What doesn't lie? Facts!

When we talk about sustainability with investments, we are not only focused on the external process of investing but the internal as well. Some investors learn the hard way, but you've got this comprehensive guide that will help you ahead of time.

Many things go through your mind when you are about to purchase a property. Most of the thoughts you entertain at that point are either about the property itself or the seller.

If you are going to succeed long-term, your decisions must be logical, facts, and numbers, not emotions. You are an investor; you are in this game to make money not to become a sympathetic buyer because a property is losing value or because you have a relationship with the seller.

This step is very crucial because no investor intentionally sets out to make an emotional investment. Emotional investments are mostly involuntary and done subconsciously. If you are a naturally empathic person, you can be in the category of investors who make such decisions.

You are trained to always check your MOTIVE for investing before appending your signature on any document. Instead of saying, "I believe that property will do well on the market," you should say, "I know the property is a great investment based on the numbers."

Belief is an emotional expression because you can believe whatever you want and the market estimations and predictions are saying something else. Some sellers may become very desperate to convince you, and they may show you what they

"Think" makes the property of value.

Instead of deciding on what they present, go with facts! Facts never lie, and numbers mean everything. Always rely on the information you garner from your research and expert opinion.

There is a lot of emphasis on this point because when you make repeated emotional decisions, you will be stuck with properties that don't bring back ROI.

Discover Your Niche

Know what you want to do, and focus on it!

When you start as an investor, you have access to a broad market, and you wouldn't know which one will become your area of expertise. So you are like a new fisherman at sea who isn't familiar with the depths and parts of the sea where the best fish live.

The more you throw your net into the deep sea, the more conversant you become with the area. The more you try markets, the more experience you garner enough to know the niche you love.

Experienced investors always encourage new investors to settle for a niche because it is a significant way of ensuring sustainability. But aside from the sustainability narrative, focusing on a niche helps you become a more focused investor.

Without a niche in mind, you will take on several deals that cut across numerous aspects of the real estate market, making you have so many insight and little control.

Investment, real, and successful venture means having a measure of control over your choices.

As an investor, you don't need to invest in every market to succeed, which is why you have the opportunity to try out as many sectors as you can so you can narrow down your choice.

Having a niche means you become passionate about every detail in that particular market. Instead of spending hours reading through multiple real estate news on all types of properties in the market, you only get to learn about what concerns your niche.

Of course, you can still keep an eye on the general market, but your focus and investment plans will be tailored to suit your niche. Over time you will discover that you have become an authority figure in that niche because you know how the market works.

Other investors who wish to delve into your niche will seek you for advice as you become the go-to person for investment counsel in a particular market. Sticking to a niche also increases your success rate with transactions because you have dedicated time to the market.

In some cases, you can predict the rate at which the market rises, falls, and appreciates. A niche offers you the mastery over a sector in a large market, and sometimes that is all you need to smash your investment goals.

Be an Investor with Integrity

Integrity in investment is a currency!

Integrity is a trait you build consciously, and it can aid multiple success for you as an investor. All through this investment journey, you will encounter people who come to you with proposals on how you can earn more through deals by doing something shady.

You will also find loopholes in contracts that will give you the liberty to cheat someone else without being exposed. You are being informed of these plausible scenarios ahead of time so you can prepare to ignore them.

Do you recall the chapter where we discussed some possible ways of investing without using any money? Well, to utilize most of those ideas, you must be a person of integrity, someone people can trust.

People wouldn't trust you because you say they should, people believe action and consistency. The real estate investor space in your country, state, or city is smaller than you think. One lousy deal from you can put a dent in your name forever.

Carry out your transactions with all sense of professionalism and ethical standards. It is better to walk away from a deal than to stick around and mess up your name.

The moment you start investing, all eyes will be on you: bankers, family, friends, other investors, landlords, realtors, etc. You may not know it, but someone is monitoring your rise as an investor, so give them an impressive show.

If you are an honest investor, believe it when I say that you can secure loans quickly. You can also take risks with other people's properties because they trust you.

Honest investors are never in a fix money-wise because everyone who aids them financially has the utmost faith in their ability to uphold details of a contract. Make up your mind today to be an honest investor who is trustworthy and reliable.

Comprehensive Yearly Plan

Planning aids vision!

Also, you need to have a comprehensive 3-5 year plan, which will become the blueprint of your investment. What this plan does is to incorporate your overall ideas with your goals as well as timelines for implementation.

For an active sustainable plan, you will need first to break your multi-year project into quarterly and annual goals. The desire to succeed may cause you to rush through the process, and this can be very overwhelming.

The rush puts a strain on you and causes you to take on too much at a time. So here is what you can do: break your plans into chunks of time you can handle while keeping the comprehensive yearly plan in mind.

Breaking down plans will enable you to track your progress easily. So you need to make adjustments to your goals when it no longer rhymes with the reality of your investment plan.

It is one thing to write a plan with deadlines, and it is another process entirely to match the program with what is happening in real-time. So don't feel bad about making certain adjustments, it is all part of the process.

You may be planning to sell a property at a specific time; your research tells you the exact time to make the high sales. But the period comes, and suddenly it seems like if you sell, it will be at a loss!

If you get to an unpredictable situation; go back to the plan and slot the sale for another time. So can you see that because you have an idea, you have everything under control (even unexpected events?)

Your comprehensive yearly plan should also entail answers to questions such as the timing for when you will purchase properties through the years.

We spoke about being intentional in a previous step, and planning is a part of intentionality.

With this yearly plan, you will be able to practice accountability!

Some investors do not hold themselves accountable, and it is a problem. You are the boss of your investment plans, so it is easy to not check on your progress. No one else will hold you accountable; so you make all of these plans without an accountability plan.

Please take all of these ideas seriously by implementing them as quickly as you can. A yearly plan is not something you can succeed without; it is essential to the grand scheme of things!

- Be realistic with your plans, yet daring
- Be bold and calculative
- Be confident and cautious with deals
- Be certain yet willing to make changes
- Be in love with the process of planning and get excited about the execution process!

Stay Hungry

Above all, sustainability is about hunger!

Not hunger for food but craving for more investment

achievements. Some people were like you years back (beginners). They had a passion for excellence with real estate investment and will consistently read books such as this until they found answers.

Well, it turned out that right after they started making some ROI, they relaxed. They erroneously assumed that the market would wait for them hence the reason for their relaxed nature.

As an investor, you've got to stay hungry, or you will become complacent, mediocre, and uninspired. Reach for higher heights of success even when you've done so well already.

The real estate market is one of the oldest and most profitable means of investments; they have been several other successful investors in the past and ahead of you.

Some older men and women have retired and completely live off the proceeds of their real estate. These older ones wouldn't have such an opportunity today if they were average investors who cared about the basics of investment.

If you are going to be a real estate investor long-term with the fantastic results to show for it, then you must stay hungry for success. Compete with yourself to outdo your past achievements and stay ahead of the game.

Every investment opportunity offers an opportunity for long term rewards. You need to know how the market works and continue to build your portfolio the right way.

When you type the keywords "Real Estate Investors in the world" from wherever you are now, you will see a list of successful individuals. These people are consistently at the top of their game as investors. You can be a part of that list; you can inspire others as well, start by staying hungry for ever-growing success.

There is so much possibility with real estate investments!

You are about to become a part of a profitable system that rewards hard work, diligence, and smart decisions. Always make sure you are thinking about sustainability at all times because it isn't what you know now that counts.

What matters is the correlation between what you know now and how it shapes your future. There is one more concluding section you must read through, and then you are ready to take over the real estate investment market.

Conclusion

Now you are ready to start investing!

The real estate market is quite a dynamic one, and the people who have great stories to tell about it are those who continuously reinvent the wheels of their investment efforts.

No goodbyes yet, it is time you show commitment by utilizing lessons gained thus far. Listen, if you put this book down now, open your browser and type in the keywords "How to become a real estate investor," you will get multiple helpful responses.

With this ease of access to information, so many people do not get it right with real estate investment. Now you have a book that contains effective strategies you wouldn't find anywhere else, would you utilize it?

The words in this book can either remain mere words to you or come alive in your world through intentional implementation. This material isn't a self-help book, and you don't have to wait for the stars to align before taking a leap and doing what is required to gain results.

It is an investment guide that teaches about a passive income idea in the most effective way. This realization means that as you read, you have to take action or else it will all be for nothing.

We started with the foundational aspects like you would get in any investment class. We then built on the foundation with ideas, suggestions, steps, and propositions that will help you get the best out of this experience.

You are through reading, well done, but the question remains what's next?

In the modern world today, having access to knowledge, or knowing something doesn't mean anything anymore. Yes, it's cool that you make an effort to read, learn, and discover, but being an investor isn't about how cool but how productive you become.

If what you learn doesn't add any value to your aspirations, then it isn't useful. So the great ideas you've got from this book must be utilized for you to experience the thrill of being a real estate investor.

Unlike other books you may have read on the subject matter, this one requires some action on your part. The more actionable steps you take, the better you become at investing.

What you have just read through is a material that can transform your entire investment career. The content in this book will help you make better decisions and place you at the forefront of innovative disruptions with real estate investment.

Be bold enough to take action, be consistent with the efforts, and you will enjoy the process. When you implement ideas, it presents an opportunity to learn new concepts. You will also unlearn the unproductive ones and relearn unique patterns that enable you to remain relevant in the investment scenes.

Of course, as mentioned throughout this book, there will be tough days when it feels like you shouldn't be taking this route because of sudden changes in the market.

But what makes you think as an investor aren't the good days with rainbows. What makes you an experienced investor is the ups and downs you go through on this journey. Do not expect rainbows all the time. (Do we even have rainbows daily in real-time?)

Be inspired by other investors by being daring, proactive, and experimental with knowledge gained. You will have the most exciting experience that helps you build a rich and diverse real estate investment portfolio.

It all begins with the first step.

Best Wishes.

References

1. Eman, H, (2019), How to Become a Real Estate Investor in 8 Easy Steps, Retrieved from https://www.mashvisor.com/blog/how-to-become-a-real-estate-investor-8-steps/

2. The Rich Dad Channel, (2017) Kiyosaki's Real Estate Investing Step By Step: How to Have Infinite Return on Your Investment, Retrieved from https://www.youtube.com/watch?v=LrSr0u_CAP8

3. Brandon, T, (n/d) Forget the MLS…Here Are 7 Clever Ways to Find Great Real Estate Deals! Retrieved from https://www.biggerpockets.com/blog/2015-02-23-forget-mls-7-clever-ways-find-great-real-estate-deals

4. Brandon, T, (2016), 3 Tips for Finding Incredible Real Estate Deals Through the MLS, Retrieved from https://www.forbes.com/sites/brandonturner/2016/09/21/3-tips-for-finding-incredible-real-estate-deals-through-the-mls/

5. On Property, (2014), The 11 Best Tips For Buying Your First Investment Property (Ep49), Retrieved from https://www.youtube.com/watch?v=v-CqZuAt3_Q

6. Brandon, C, (2019), What Happens on Closing day for the

Home Buyer? Retrieved from, http://www.homebuyinginstitute.com/closing.php

7. Samuel, L, (2019), Lease Option Agreement, What is a Lease Option? Retrieved from https://www.google.com/search?q=how+to+use+lease+option+agreement&oq=how+to+use+lease+option+agreement&aqs=chrome..69i57.9863j0j7&sourceid=chrome&ie=UTF-8#kpvalbx=_RY5AXa6uHbKqrgTO96uoDg28

8. Amy, F, (2019), The Ins and Outs of Seller-financed Real Estate Deals, Retrieved from https://www.investopedia.com/articles/mortgages-real-estate/10/should-you-use-seller-financing.asp

www.ingramcontent.com/pod-product-compliance
Lightning Source LLC
Chambersburg PA
CBHW070648220526
45466CB00001B/349